Secrets of the Caribbean Islands

Cayman Islands

Secrets of the Caribbean Islands

Cayman Islands

How to invest in Real Estate and Business

Andrea Hoff-Domin

1.   Edition 2015—English

Photographs by Florida Services & Information LLC

Map by Microsoft map point

Cover photograph by Florida Services & Information LLC, Fort Lauderdale, Florida

ISBN: 0986252921

ISBN-13: 978-0-9862529-2-1

National Motto of the Cayman Islands

He hath founded it upon the seas.

About the Author

Born in lower Saxony, Germany, Andrea Hoff-Domin lost her father when she was a baby, and life with her new stepfather was never easy. Books about foreign countries and their cultures were her escape from everyday life and inspired her enthusiasm for the wide world. Her grandparents, especially her grandfather, had a big influence on her. He was an architect, and she accompanied him on his trips to construction sites and sat at his feet when he was drawing houses. At that time, she developed her passion for houses and properties, which is her main profession today.

She runs an international brokerage in Florida and is known as a Florida expert. To fulfill her lifelong dream, she started her career as a financial specialist in the biggest German bank and renovated condominiums. During that time, she began to write for several magazines and Internet portals. She lives by the motto "Do or do not; there is no try" (Yoda, *Star Wars*).

www.florida-dream-homes.net
www.andreahoffdomin.com
andrea@florida-informations.com

Contents

Why Cayman Islands?

That is a very good question, one we also asked ourselves. I had heard about these islands during my own work at the banking data center in Germany when I managed the electronic foreign currency reports for the government regulation reports However, I had only a vague knowledge of where these islands were.

The islands have already been on the tourism industry's routes for a long time, but as a cruise ship passenger, you are normally not really interested in the geographic locations of the stops on your journey. You certainly enjoy all the adventures on the cruise ship or at your destinations more.

You surely know all the amusing pirate stories like the *Pirates of the Caribbean*, and you love the adventure and the romance of the pirate's life. However, do you know where these pirates were at home? Do you know where they stopped for food and water and to repair their ship? Maybe or maybe not.

It was the same with us. We have lived in Florida, just at the entrance to the Caribbean Sea, for years. We love Florida; however, understanding it never hurts to expand our horizons, we explore our next-door Caribbean neighbors.

Our goal on our exploring tours is to discover real estate and business opportunities in the Caribbean Sea region and to provide our information and research results to our customers. This information helps them find and realize their own Caribbean adventure goals in one of these countries, and it will do the same for you.

This book focuses on the Cayman Islands and gives you vital details about the real estate and business opportunities they offer. The information is as accurate as possible, but for deeper evaluation of your individual situation, we recommend checking with professional service providers like local attorneys and accountants.

Accompany us on the discovery tour of these tropical islands in the Caribbean Sea, with their underwater wonderlands and excellent offshore business opportunities in a tax-neutral environment.

In this book you will see a detailed picture of the British overseas territory, along with its immigration, economy, government, and real estate. We are sure that you will love the islands and come for a visit. Maybe you'll like it so much that you decide to stay.

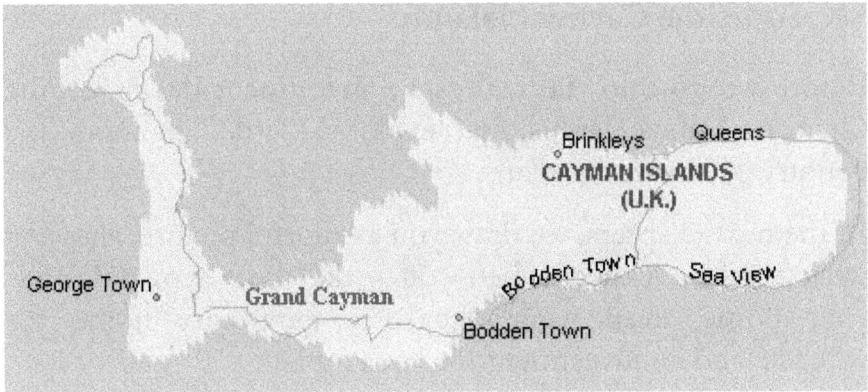

Grand Cayman Island

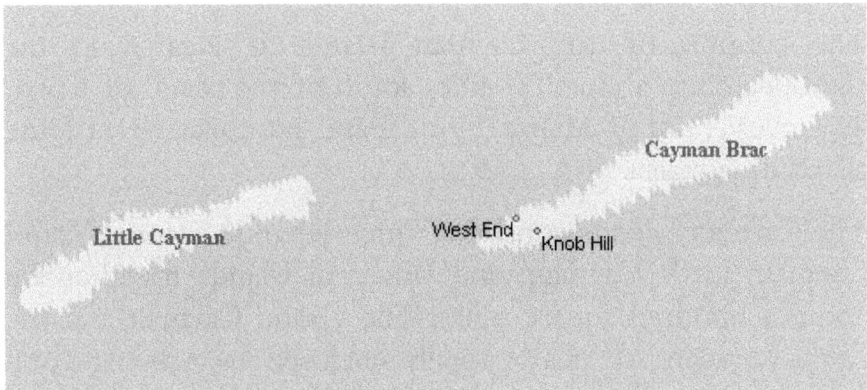

The islands Little Cayman and Brac

Secrets of the Cayman Islands

Before we go into the real estate investment details of the Cayman Islands, let us first explore a little bit about the country of the Caymanians.

In the next chapters, we draw you a colorful picture, showing what you can expect when you make the Cayman Islands your home, even when they're a temporary home for yourself and an investment for your money.

Geography

The country of the Cayman Islands is located in the Caribbean Sea, about 150 miles south of the island of Cuba; 460 miles south of Miami, Florida; and 180 miles west of the island of Jamaica.

The Cayman Islands consist of three separate islands: Grand Cayman, Little Cayman, and Brac. All islands together are about a hundred square miles. The Grand Cayman and the Little Cayman are nearly totally enclosed by a living coral reef. These reefs attract many kinds of fish and make the islands one of the most famous diving areas in the world.

The islands are the peaks of underwater mountains, which are part of a ridge that stretches from the southeast of Cuba close to the shoreline of Belize. The underwater mountain ridge is the northern rim of the Cayman Trench, which, with a depth of twenty-five thousand feet, is the deepest point in the Caribbean Sea. The trough is also the friction line between the North American and Caribbean Plates. Jamaica, the next-door neighbor, is only 180 miles to the east and sits on the opposite side of the underwater trench.

Because the Cayman Islands are the highest points of these underwater mountains, they have no natural freshwater rivers and valleys for the water runoff. This missing water runoff makes the water around the islands crystal clear and an excellent habitat for corals and tropical fish.

The fresh water on the island is extracted from salt water, which is taken from wells in the limestone, and is afterward treated to make it drinkable. The other available water source is the collected rain water, but this water is mostly used for yards.

The smaller islands—Little Cayman and Brac—are vacation posts, where you can enjoy the quietness and the pure nature around you like Robinson Cruso.

When you speak about the Cayman Islands, you often refer only to Grand Cayman. The action happens on this island, and most business is done here. These businesses ensure the prosperity of the country and are detailed further in the following chapters.

The island Grand Cayman has three tiers. The highest tier is the island itself. Its highest point is 60 feet (18 m) above sea level and, as already mentioned, is the peak of an underwater mountain. The length of the island is 22 miles (35 km), and the widest stretch is 8 miles (13 km). The average width is 4 miles (6.5 km), and at its smallest areas—like Seven Miles Beach—the width is slighty a mile.

1 foot = 0.3048 m

1 mile = 1.609 km

The second tier is the area within the surrounding coral reef. This reef nearly encloses the whole island and is like a protection barrier for the lagoon between West Bay and Rum Point. Within this reef the water is relatively shallow and offers excellent diving and snorkeling spots to observe fish and explore the numerous shipwrecks that lie on the seafloor.

The lagoon that is located between the west and east part of the island is called North Sound. In this lagoon you have the opportunity to see and learn many details about the nature of the area. You can swim and play with the gentle stingrays, observe and touch the starfish, and much more.

The third tier is localized beyond the coral reef, and there the water depth is growing fast. This area is also called the Cayman wall or Cayman drop, and it leads on the south side of Cayman to the deepest point of the Caribbean Sea: the Cayman Trench.

This geographic structure offers many benefits to the Cayman Islands' economy because it attracts tourists, and tourism is one of the main industries in the country. The visitors come either by cruise ship or aircraft to enjoy the sun and the pristine waters, with its underwater wonders and above-water treasures.

Climate

The Cayman Islands belong climatically to the tropics, and there are some specifics you should know.

The location within the tropics means that the islands are closer to the equator, so day- and nighttime are nearly equal the whole year around. Based on this fact, there is no daylight saving change in the Cayman Islands like in other countries across the world.

For instance, during the wintertime, Cayman lives in the Eastern Standard Time (EST), the same as Miami, and the time difference to London is five hours.

When the United States and European countries change to daylight saving time, the time in the Cayman Islands stays the same. The only difference is that time now matches with the US Central Standard Time. The difference from Miami is one hour and from the United Kingdom is now six hours.

This information is important when you are doing business with others from across the world. When you come to Cayman, the airlines have already factored this information into their airline ticket and flight information.

With the location in the tropics also come the mild swings in temperature. During the year the temperature sways between 72 and 88°F, or 22 and 31°C.

The tropics also get the most rain in comparison to the other climate zones, and the rain is mostly concentrated in the summer months. The rain showers are heavy and usually short in time. During the rain pours, flooding is possible.

The high tourist season for Cayman is during the winter months from November to March. In those months the temperatures swing between 72 and 80°F, and showers are less intense.

During the summer months—May to October—the temperatures sway between 80 and 88°F. That is the rainy season with heavy downpours and high humidity. The hottest months are July and August.

The pristine and crystal-clear water has a year-around water temperature between 78 and 85°F, and it is always a pleasure to jump into the waves for a swim, snorkel, or dive adventure.

As already mentioned the Cayman Islands are located in the tropics and are within the hurricane zone. That means that between June 1 and November 30, the possiblity of a hurricane exists. However, a direct hurricane hit is rare. The last big hurricane was Ivan in 2004.

Based on this information, you can expect a tropical paradise with much sun and gentle breezes, swaying palm trees, and white sandy beaches with shady trees and blue-green shimmering waves.

Sunscreen for your skin protection is a good idea along with a light sweater for indoors. The humidity makes it necessary that your home be air-conditioned year-round.

There are no health risks on the islands like malaria or dengue fever, and you don't need any vaccinations for your stay. No dangerous or life-threatening animals live on the islands, although some plants and insect bites can provoke an allergic reaction that may need treatment. Antihistamine cream or gel is a good aid against the itching in such a case.

When you are allergic or sensitive to mosquito bites, an insect repellent is a good idea to use in the evening hours or after a heavy rainpour because, at those moments, the mosquitos come for dinner.

When you come for a visit, you should have travel health insurance, or you should check with your health insurance provider at home to see if and to what extent you are covered abroad. You are liable for your health expenses in Cayman and for paying your medical costs out of pocket. There is no direct reimbursement or billing with your health care provider at home.

Flora of the Cayman Islands

The term *flora* describes the specific plants and vegetation in a particular region, in this case Cayman. There are some particularities that are important for this island and that influence the living.

On the east side of the North Sound—the lagoon—you will find a mangrove area. These mangroves have some interesting features. They are growing in salt water but can desalinate the water that they need for their survival.

The mangroves filter the salt out of the water and collect it in their leaves, which turn yellow and fall off. These falling leaves are the first step to becoming soil later on.

During a tropical storm, the mangroves offer protection against the storm surge, and some boaters use the mangroves as a natural safe haven during a storm. In normal weather conditions, the mangroves are a rainmaker for the island.

Another very important plant in the Cayman Islands is the silver thatch palm tree. This palm is also the national tree of the country.

This palm tree was and is to this day a natural resource for typical Cayman products. The tree's leaves are very strong and durable and were used to produce ropes for sailing ships, brooms, and everyday items like plaited bags, hats, and baskets. These plaited products are still sold and in use on the islands. You can buy them at farmers' markets, for example at Camana Bay, and in some local shops.

The palm tree leaves were also an excellent building material for the houses and Cayman outdoor kitchens, the so-called caboose. An example of such a building you can see is Perdo Saint James.

Another national plant is the wild banana orchid. This orchid beauty has white petals with purple lips, and you can find it in the trees in the woodland areas. The best location to see this national treasure is in the Queen Elizabeth II Botanic Garden, in the Orchid Broadway.

Fauna of the Cayman Islands

The island-specific vegetation in the swamp and the mangroves is an excellent environment to protect the fauna of the island like iguanas and birds, but also the not-so-welcome mosquitos.

The mosquitos were a plague in the past, and you had to use a mosquito net around your bed at night or a smoke pot in your rooms to keep the mean little insects out of your home.

Today this plague is under control with the usage of environmentally safe methods, and the mosquitos bother you only during the twilight time or after a heavy rain shower or when you walk through woodland areas on the eastern portion of Cayman.

One of the national animals is the Cayman parrot. This parrot is a beautiful green bird with red cheeks and blue tail and wing feathers. It lives in the woodlands and the black mangroves, and when you go on bird watch, you can hear it chatting. You can also find the bird by simply visiting the Botanic Garden.

There are two other animals that are endangered and special to the Cayman Islands: the green sea turtles and the blue iguana.

The turtles were always a treasure of the islands. They are an excellent protein producer, and in former times sailors hunted them as a meat source on their journeys. The extreme hunting nearly wiped them out and was banned in 1988.

In 1968 the Turtle Farm was established in Cayman to breed the green sea turtles. These bred sea turtles are released into the wild as soon as they are mature enough to survive. Some of the bred turtles are sold to local restaurants because their meat is a local delicacy.

The blue iguana is also called the Grand Cayman iguana. This lizard lives in the sunlit, open, rocky areas of the dry wood regions and in the Botanic Garden.

This species was nearly extinct, and in 2005 only three individual iguanas were left in the wild. With a managed breeding program, it was possible to increase the blue iguana population living in the wild to 750 individuals in 2012, and today this species is no longer critically endangered, but still endangered nonetheless.

Blue iguana – Cayman species

The green iguanas that you can find everywhere on the island are invaders to the area and are not protected.

In the open waters around the island, you often find friendly fish and beautiful corals that you can enjoy on a diving or snorkeling trip. However, you should never touch a coral because it will die.

The same is true for fish. It is safer only watching the fish than touching them, especially jellyfish and lionfish, as well as the sea urchin, which can hurt you with its pikes and leave you feeling a nasty itch after the sting. You can treat these stings with vinegar or antihistamine cream.

This is only a small selection of the plants and animals of the Cayman Islands. To find more information on this topic, the Botanic Garden and the many organized adventure boat tours are excellent resources.

Time Travel through the Islands' History

Before Christopher Columbus discovered Little Cayman and Brac as the first European visitor on May 10, 1503, the islands were already known and visited by travelers from the West Indies, who were very good mariners.

When Columbus set foot on the islands, he discovered they were filled with turtles and named them Las Tortugas, which means *turtles*. In the Cayman Islands, this date is still a national holiday and is celebrated on the third Monday in May each year.

At that time the islands were known for their turtle population, crocodiles, alligators, and iguanas, which the sailors hunted for food. The seamen also found fresh water for their journey in the rainwater ponds.

Until 1660 the Cayman Islands stayed nearly empty and were only occupied by turtles, alligators, and lizards. From time to time, pirates came by to plunder Spanish ships, stock up their food supplies, and repair their own ships.

The golden age of piracy was between 1650 and 1730. At that time pirates like Blackbeard and Morgan were frequent visitors to the islands. They came here not only for food and water but also to recruit seamen from the captured Spanish ships.

This pirate spirit is still alive in today's Cayman Islands and is celebrated each year in November during Pirate's Week.

In 1670 the Spanish and the British signed the Treaty of Madrid, and with this contract Spain acknowledged the possessions of the British Crown in the Caribbean. As a part of this treaty, the island of Jamaica and the Cayman Islands became a part of the British Empire.

Another part of this agreement was that the British would suppress piracy in the Caribbean, and from that time on, pirates were in the sights of the British, as we all know from the Pirates of the Caribbean movies. The main authority and jurisdiction were located in Jamaica, and the Cayman Islands were a dependency of Jamaica.

In 1730 the first settlement was built on the Cayman Islands. The settlers during that time were mostly soldiers who had fled from Jamaica.

In 1780 the British settler William Eden came to Grand Cayman to establish his cotton and mahogany plantation. At that time mahogany trees were one of the most used building materials in the Caribbean because of their strength. At the home of William Eden—the so-called Pedro Saint James Castle—you can see the building was constructed from this fine wood.

Today the mahogany trees are rare and protected. The cutting of such a tree is illegal and punished with a six-figure fine or several years in prison.

The Pedro Saint James Castle is the oldest building on Cayman, and it has survived even the strongest hurricanes. This landmark building and its surrounding garden are today a museum and event location for public and private functions.

In the census of 1802, only 933 people lived on Grand Cayman. Half of them were British settlers, and the other half were slaves. Already at that time, the islands were a tax-free zone because the settlers on the island produced very little beyond their personal needs, and that little was not taxable.

The first gathering of the representatives of the five Cayman districts was in 1831 in Pedro Saint James Castle, and the first election for this assembly was on December 31, 1831. At that time the Cayman Islands had two thousand inhabitants, and the islands still officially had slavery.

In 1835 the governor of Jamaica came to Pedro Saint James Castle, which was always used for public purposes in Cayman at that time, and declared the end of slavery based on the Emancipation of the Brish West Indies and the Slavery Abolition Act of 1833.

Between 1830 and 1840, the first missionaries came to Grand Cayman and built the first schools. One of these mission homes can still be visited, although you need an appointment for the interior visit. This mission house is located in Bodden Town, the first capital of the country.

Over the next hundred years, the Cayman Islands enjoyed the Caribbean sun and lifestyle by themselves. In 1937 the first cruise ships discovered the islands as a vacation place, and slowly Cayman became a spot on the map. However, the real tourism industry started in the 1950s with a few hotels and diving companies.

Besides the cruise ships, there was a seaplane service that connected Grand Cayman to the rest of the world. In 1953 the first airfield opened on the island and replaced the former seaplane service. The national airline Cayman Airways began its service in 1968.

Also in 1953, the first hospital and the first commercial bank opened their doors to the public.

The next step on the way to independence was the first written constitution in 1959. This constitution granted voting rights to women and terminated the islands' dependency to Jamaica.

In 1962, when Jamaica got its independence from the United Kingdom, the Cayman Islands decided to stay connected as a Crown colony. Today this status is called an overseas territory.

A new constitution was written in 1972. Since that time the Cayman Islands have become governed by the legislative assembly, the executive council, and a governor. The governor is appointed by the government of the United Kingdom.

In the same year, the Cayman Islands established their own currency: the Cayman Islands dollar, or KYD. The Cayman dollar is only used in the Cayman Islands, but you can also pay everywhere locally with US dollars. The conversion from US dollar to Cayman dollar can be done in every store, restaurant, or bank because the exchange rate is fixed. Therefore, it is not necessary to shop around for the best rate. Details on this topic are in the financing chapter.

With the establishment of these pillars, the foundation for the most important industry in the Cayman Islands was set: the financial and banking industry. This industry thrives within the tax-free zone of the islands and attracts many globally active banks—international law and accounting experts who serve their customers with their offshore business transactions.

Regarding the tax-free status of the islands, there is a little story to know. In 1794 ten British ships sank in Gun Bay at the east end of Cayman, but all crew members and passengers were rescued. A royal prince was among the passengers pulled from the water, and because of his rescue, the king made the decree that the island should be forever tax-free. This is one of the most popular stories in Cayman, and you will hear it everywhere, but sadly that story is only a legend.

The real reason for the tax-free status is that there was nothing to tax in former times, and the tax-neutral status of the Cayman Islands has been kept to this day. This status means that there is no income tax, no inheritance tax, no sales tax, no corporation capital gains tax, no property tax, and no tax withholdings for any other governments in the Cayman Islands.

Besides the financial industry, the other major industry, tourism, took off in 1970. In that year there were only 403 visitors on the islands, and today there are 1.7 million tourists coming to Grand Cayman each year. They arrive either by air or cruise ship.

While in former times the pirates were a threat to these islands' populations and the British authorities, this is not the case nowadays. The Cayman Islands are the safest islands within the Caribbean and have an extremely low crime rate.

The connection to the United Kingdom is still visible in the flag of the Cayman Islands. The flag that flies on land has a blue background with the Union Jack in the upper left corner, and the nation's coat of arms is placed in a white circle on the right half of the flag. This coat of arms is the short version of the Cayman Islands' history. It illustrates the former dependency to Jamaica and today's status as an overseas territory, as well as its national treasures: the water and the turtles.

When the flag flies on the sea, it contains the same symbols, but the background is red.

Cayman Islands Flag

Culture Respect to the Caymanians

When you are on the Cayman Islands, please keep in mind that you are a guest in a foreign country and that the Cayman population has a different cultural background and experience than you do. The best way to make friends and feel comfortable is to observe and adapt your personal behavior during your stay on the islands.

The people of Cayman are always polite and respectful to you. When you meet them on the street, they will greet you with "Good morning," or "Good afternoon." That is the best way to start a conversation.

If you know the first name of your conversation partner, you can include a "Miss" or "Mister" before the name. That is a respectful way of addressing a person.

As mentioned earlier, the Cayman Islands do not have daylight saving time. That means that when you are, for example, from New York and are on the islands during the winter months, then you do not need to adjust your watch. When you are in the Caymans during the summer months, then you have to turn your watch back one hour, because in New York there is daylight saving time but not in the Caymans.

The usual business hours for shops and other service providers are 8:30 a.m. to 5:00 p.m. on weekdays. Some businesses operate on Saturdays, too, but have different opening hours. On Sundays all businesses are closed. You cannot shop on Sundays, as you may be used to in your home country.

Restaurants close usually at 10:00 or 11:00 p.m., and bars shut their doors at midnight or 1:00 a.m. at the latest. The gratitude for the service in restaurants and bars is often included and added to your check. You will find a note at the bottom of your check that states the amount of the gratitude. If the gratitude is not included, the common amount for gratitude is 15 percent of the check balance.

The Caymanians have no income or sales tax, but the state has to generate income. To do so, the hotels and other tourism services have to collect a tourist tax, which is 13 percent of the invoice amount.

When you go shopping, please keep in mind, haggling is not common in Cayman because you do not have to pay sales tax as you often do in your home country. There are also many articles on sale, and to haggle will out you as a tourist and will not give you any more savings.

In the islands you can choose between all kinds of food from all parts of the world. The restaurants offer international cuisine and specialities. However, when you are here, you should prefer the local cuisine.

The typical local food is seafood and fish as well as chicken—roasted or cooked—and turtle burger. Traditional dishes are conch stew and fish rundown, often spicy and hot, and for dessert rum cake with raisins. You will not always find these dishes in the large restaurants but in the small local ones.

You are on a tropical island, and in such a location, watching the sunset with a tropical cocktail in your hand and a dinner at the waterfront or on the sandy beach is the best way to enjoy your evenings. The Cayman Islands offer these opportunities at several places, along with additional sunset entertainment like salsa lessons or Caribbean music.

The music is influenced by the European and African ancestry of the Cayman Island. It has its own rhythm and its own lyrics. The music is similar to folk music and is presented at select places on the island from local musicians. In the bars you usually will hear the common modern dance music.

When you are on Cayman, you may wonder about the chickens that are running with their baby chickens all over the place. They are feral chickens and live everywhere. They are shy and will run away when you try to touch them. In the morning hours, you can often hear a rooster calling for his family.

The country is a business headquarters for offshore businesses and transactions, banks, and expatriates. Due to this the dress code is casual fashion. That means women wear skirts and blouses or dresses during the day. For men a shirt and a long pair of trousers is the right choice. During a black tie event, a cocktail dress—long or short—for the ladies and a dinner jacket for the gentlemen is the way to go.

Often you will see people in swimwear on public streets. They are often tourists from the cruise ships and do not know any better. It is disrespectful to the Cayman people to walk in swimwear along the roads. Therefore, please put on a sun dress or shorts with a top when you are on your way to public beaches.

At the public beaches, topless sunbathing or nudity is strictly forbidden, and it is good guest manners to respect these rules and cover your personal treasures.

The Caymanians are strongly family oriented, and on the weekends they enjoy their leisure time by gathering on the porch or under a big shady tree in the yard. You will often see them talking about their favorite topics or the newest neighborhood gossip, or playing dominos with a cool drink in their hands.

Another kind of entertainment is the picnic at the beaches on the weekends or holidays. The whole family enjoys the day under a shady tree on the sandy beach. Another traditional habit is the land crab hunting during the rainy season.

This all together shows that the Caribbean charm of the past still exists, and the Cayman Islands are still a bit as they were described: the islands that time forgot.

Country Products

Since the first settlers came to the islands, the main products have come from the land, the plants, and the animals of Cayman.

The most important products, which are still famous today, are the bags, baskets, and hats. They are woven from the leaves of the silver thatch palm trees, and tourists love them. There are only a few persons on the island who know the art of making these products.

During the time of the sail ships, ropes made from the silver thatch palm leaves were well liked and taken because of their durability and strength.

The turtle hunting for the meat was a great source of income for the Caymanians. This excessive hunting of these animals nearly destroyed the green sea turtle population. In 1988 the hunting of wild green sea turtles was banned by the Cayman government. When you want to hunt a green sea turtle, you have to get a license for the hunting to prevent punishment. The interest for this hunting is very small, and there were no hunting permits issued in the last couple of years.

Today the green sea turtles are bred at the Turtle Farm in Cayman. The eggs are taken from the breeding beach and put into an incubator. When the turtles hatch and are strong enough to survive in the open waters, they are released into the Caribbean Sea.

The meat of the sea turtles is a delicacy on the Cayman Islands, and you can taste these dishes in some small local restaurants. You can be sure that this meat is bred at the Turtle Farm and from wild hunted sea turtle.

Other activities in the former days were ship building, sponge harvesting, wrecking, guano collecting, and shark hunting for the leather industry, as well as operating hardwood plantations with mahogany and cedar trees.

All these products were used for the exchange of other necessary goods for the Caymanians, like clothes, sugar, and kerosene.

The above products are replaced with today's modern products, like tamarind candies and homemade jellies and jams from peppers and chilies, as well as spicy hot sauces.

Salt water soap, rum cakes, and jewelry made from Caymanite are also nice memories or gifts from the Cayman Islands.

You can buy these products at the local farmers' markets, which are held at different locations on the islands and in many local stores.

Transportation and Driving in the Cayman Islands

When you are on the Cayman Islands, you have different options to go from point A to point B. The easiest way is to drive by yourself. However, you need to keep in mind, this is an overseas territory of the United Kingdom, and the traffic rules are based on the British driving rules and habits.

You have to drive on the left side of the road, and that can be tough at first, especially when you are from a country where you drive on the right side of the road.

With this left-side driving come some traffic rules that you seriously must keep in mind and follow to prevent an accident.

You often have a middle lane in the roads, and this lane is only for turning right onto a different road or into a property entrance. Never use this lane for passing slow traffic, because that will quickly cause an accident.

When you come to a four-way stop, the cars drive as they arrive. That means the car that arrives first, drives first. Please be cautious when you look at the car's turn signal; not every driver is perfect in showing his or her direction. You as the driver also have to adjust to your car's instruments. When your car has the steering wheel on the right side, the turning signal and the window wipers are reversed, and that can be very confusing at the beginning.

In the Cayman Islands, there are many roundabouts to direct traffic. You enter into such a roundabout clockwise and have to give way to the traffic that is already in the roundabout.

There are also some regulations you should follow strictly. Otherwise, you will risk hefty fines.

- Seatbelts are mandatory while driving.

- Texting or speaking on a cell phone is prohibited.

- Driving over the speed limit and drinking while driving are prohibited.

These are simple rules, and everybody knows them because they do not only apply in the Cayman Islands but in many other countries, too. The bigger issue is that you must always keep in mind to drive on the left side of the road, and that can be a stress factor when you drive while intoxicated.

When you rent a car in Cayman, you need a valid driver's license from your home country. This driver's license will be transferred to a temporary Cayman visitor driver's license for the term of your stay or your rental period—whatever applies best.

Such a visitor driver's license is issued directly from your rental car company, and it usually costs twenty Cayman dollars.

When you are the driver and younger than twenty-one years old, then you might have some problems renting a car at all, and you have to purchase full coverage insurance for your rental period.

When you stay longer than six months in the Cayman Islands, you need to get a permanent driver's license from the government after you have taken a written test. This permanent driver's license is valid for three years.

When you feel uncomfortable to drive on your own, you can use a taxi service. The taxis are often bigger vans. They are the only option for you to go to your hotel besides the rental car, because there are no free airport shuttle services to the hotels.

The government does not allow a shuttle service, but on the other hand, they also regulate the taxi fares. That means for you that there is a fixed rate to take you, for example, from the airport to Seven Miles Beach. This trip will cost you around fifteen Cayman dollars, and this price is good for one to three passengers and baggage. For each additional person in the taxi, there is an added fee of eight Cayman dollars.

There is also a minimum fee of eight Cayman dollars per person when you drive fewer than 2.2 km.

Another transportation option is the local bus system; however, such buses are not allowed in the direct airport area. These buses have a similar size to a taxi and can transport fifteen passengers.

There are nine bus routes that are operated on Grand Cayman, and they connect the western and eastern portions of the island with Georgetown.

These local bus routes have no fixed schedule, but as a rule of thumb, a bus passes by every ten minutes. You do not even have to be at a bus stop to take the bus. When you walk along the road and wave, the bus will stop and you can get in.

Sometimes while you are walking along the road, you will hear a short honk behind you. That is a local bus that is asking if you would like to have a ride. You can either flag the bus and get it or let it go.

The fare for this transport is two Cayman dollars per person, and you pay the fare when you get out of the bus.

This is the cheapest way to go around in Grand Cayman without having to drive, and it is the best chance to get in contact with the locals.

Last but not least, you can also ride a bicycle, but you have to keep in mind the traffic regulations. Bicycles do not have any privileges on the road, and you must be careful. And the walkways are for the pedestrians, not for bicycles.

There are only a few bicycle lanes, and you have to drive in the road with the cars. Riding against the traffic direction, because you hope the oncoming traffic participants can see you better, is illegal.

It does not matter which kind of transportation you choose, the pedestrians always have the highest priority in traffic, so do not drive aggressively, and always let pedestrians pass first.

Attractions and Entertainment in the Cayman Islands

Before you decide to reside and buy a property or start a business in the Cayman Islands, you certainly want to know what else you will find here.

To give you an idea of what to expect, we put together a selection of events and important landmarks in the country. This will give you a clear picture of the beauty of this tropical island.

Cultural Events

There are several interesting cultural events on Grand Cayman Island that you should know so you can plan your trip. The below selection is limited because there are so many each month, and they are constantly changing and having new ones added.

Art and Craft

Throughout the year you will find several art and craft events, where you can buy local paintings, photography, and jewelry. The local artists are often selling their products at local farmers' markets and other local events. Once a year there is an award presented to a local artist for his or her work. To win this award, the artist's work has to contribute to the art and heritage of the Cayman Islands.

One of these events is the Cayfest, which is not only known for its art and photography exhibits but also for competitions, dance, and music presentation.

The Cayfilm Cayman International Film Festival is in June each year and promotes the Cayman Islands as a world class filming spot for all kinds of productions. International celebrities and filmmakers are on Grand Cayman, and you can participate in film screenings and workshops as well as ask your questions during information sessions.

In November there is the International Storytelling Festival. Many storytellers and poets from all over the world come to the island for this event and present their art. Besides the storytelling there are many other entertainments, and there is no admission charge for the event.

Food and Wine

There are several food and wine festivals over the year. Some of these cooking events are focused on the local dishes that are prepared and presented during this function by the many restaurants and food suppliers on the Cayman Islands.

Once a year there is the Cayman Cookout, where not only local chefs show their culinary and cocktail skills, but also international chefs, sommeliers, and spirit blenders.

Each year in October is Restaurant Month, where many of the island restaurants offer their specialty menus for lower fixed prices and give you the opportunity to get a taste of their culinary art.

You will discover many interesting dishes that tickle your tastebuds.

Family and Fun Events

Throughout the year there are several events where grown-ups and little ones have fun the same way.

Once a year the Rotary club organizes its Bed Race, where the participants have to run with their own uniquely constructed bed down a main road. This is a fund-raiser event for a polio cure.

Another fun event each year in May is the Cayman Carnival Batabano. During this time you dress up with colorful costumes and many, many feathers. Everyone can participate in the parades and in the many contests or only enjoy the party and feel the tropical flair. The highlight of this event is the adult parade along the entire Seven Miles Beach stretch toward Georgetown. The children have their own smaller parade in Camana Bay.

Batabano parade

On the first Monday in July each year is Constitution Day in the Cayman Islands. On this date the islands celebrate their latest constitution with the United Kingdom. The last and actual constitution was approved by Queen Elizabeth II in June 2009.

With this official holiday, the constitution week starts, and throughout this week the constitution is on display for the residents in various libraries, and the population can address their questions about the constitution to government personnel.

Like in many other countries, Halloween is the most important event during the month of October. One of the main attractions in Cayman is the Halloween Spooktacular in Camana Bay, which offers fun for the whole family.

As mentioned earlier the Cayman Islands were a hiding place for pirates in the past, and each year in November, the pirate tradition rises again with a pirate invasion—street festivals with music and dancing, float parades, and fireworks. When you are interested in getting the pirate feeling, this is the time of the year to be here.

The year's end tradition in Cayman is the annual Christmas Tree Lighting in Camana Bay. During that time this shopping and entertainment place transforms into a sparkling Christmas wonderland with Santa Claus and Christmas carol singing.

One of the spectaculars is the boat parade with illuminated and Christmasy-decorated private boats at the waterfronts either in Georgetown or Camana Bay.

On December 31 the year ends with the traditional New Year's fireworks at the Camana Bay.

This is a limited selection of the events in the Cayman Islands with the focus on family, fun, food, art, and craft. The sporting events are listed in the wellness and sport chapter of this book.

Museums

In comparison to many other countries, the Cayman Islands are a young nation. Their written history begins when the Europeans discovered this part of the Caribbean Sea and the islands therein. The early settlers who were citizens from European countries started the writing of history.

These conquerers explored the undiscovered territory and delivered reports to their superiors about their findings. Based on these findings, the European empires determined how many taxes they could get and how many armed forces they had to send to their new possession in the New World for protection.

The history of the Cayman Islands starts with their discovery by Christopher Columbus in 1503. From these early days and the days before the discovery, there are no remains left on the islands. Today's historic sites on the islands are from the time when the British Empire was in governmental power in Jamaica and the Cayman Islands.

Pedro Saint James Castle

The oldest existing structure in Cayman is the historic site of Pedro Saint James Castle. The building was constructed with heavy limestones in 1780 by William Eden. The building has eighteen-inch-thick walls with surrounding mahogany verandas.

The house has a quarterly shape with three stories like a tower. Instead of windows allowing sunlight into the house, there are doors on each home side of the house. These doorways can be closed with strong wooden doors. These doors are also an excellent protection against the tropical storms that can blow over the island during hurricane season.

The inside of the house is a little tight for a family, but the second and third floors expand and are surrounded by beautiful mahogany verandas. These verandas offered additional living space.

On the site is a garden with fruit trees and crop plants that were cultivated in the eighteenth century and an outdoor kitchen, the so-called caboose. The preparation of the meals in this outdoor kitchen protected the main house against possible fire, and the cooking heat was easily diffused into the open air.

This historic site also played an important role in the Cayman Islands' history. The first elected parliament met there in 1831, and in 1835 the end of slavery was announced on the outside stairway.

Today this location is not only a museum but also a famous spot for weddings and social events.

Airy mahogany veranda

Cayman National Museum

This museum is close to the harbor and the tourist landing area in Georgetown. It is located in the Old Court Building and is one of the main landmarks of Grand Cayman. Its direct neighborhood to the cruise ship terminal invites many cruise ship visitors for a tour.

In the museum you will find exhibits of national heritage documents and artifacts from the Cayman Islands. The centerpiece of the museum is the artifact collection of a local resident, Mr. Ira Thompson, and a three-dimensional map of the geologic formation of the Cayman Islands.

There are more than eight thousand artifacts on display, and you will see small exhibits like coins up to big pieces like a catboat. All showpieces have a close and direct connection to the Cayman art, natural history, and island tradition.

Mission House in Bodden Town

Bodden Town was a small fishing town and the first capital on the Cayman Islands in the 1800s. This settlement did not have solidly constructed houses, so the close-by Pedro Saint James Castle became the important place for all important governmental matters.

Today there is only one heritage building left in Bodden Town—the Mission House. It is hidden and hard to find when you do not see the sign. In the 1700s the Mission House was known for its waterfowl and water supply. That made it an excellent spot for the Presbyterian missionaries in the1800s to build their traditional Cayman house and establish the Presbyterian ministry and school in Cayman.

The house is now a museum where you can get a historic glimpse into the living conditions of the 1800s. You can walk around the historic site and sit on the bench at the nearby pond, but you need to make an appointment to take the inside tour.

Cayman Motor Museum

One of the newer museums is the Cayman Motor Museum. The owner of this museum has a large private collection of exotic automobiles and motorcycles that he would like to share with more people than only his friends.

Therefore, he built his Cayman Motor Museum in West Bay, where he displays his eighty vehicles. The oldest car is a Cadillac from 1905.

Another famous exhibit is the original Bat Mobile from the TV series *Batman* in the 1960s. You will also see cars from celebrities, like the Daimler of Queen Elizabeth II. In the collection you will find luxury cars like Maserati, Corvette, Jaguar, and Rolls Royse.

His newest additions to the museum exhibit are speed boats.

The Motor Museum has speed boats too

Natural Preserves

There are many natural treasures to discover on Grand Cayman. To get a slight impression of what to expect, find here a little selection:

Beaches

The most important natural assets are the powdery, sandy beaches with the crystal-clear water. Often the wide beaches have nice big palm trees and hammocks that offer shade and protect against the heat. On Sundays you will meet many locals at the beaches having picnics.

Some beaches are smaller bays that are surrounded by limestones so that the incoming waves are slowed down. The beaches are inviting, and you can relax in the shade of a big tree or go for a nice swim or a snorkeling trip.

Access to the beaches is often small walkways between houses, and they are marked with brown signs with *Beach Access* printed on them.

Beach view

Queen Elizabeth II Botanic Garden

One of the most prestigious natural preserves on the Cayman Islands is the Botanic Garden. This park was opened in 1994. It is sixty-five acres and consists of a walking trail through the dry woodland forest as well as the nicely planted park.

The park has several gardens, a lake, and wetlands for the wildlife. In the heritage garden, you will find an old Caymanian house with a typical sand front yard and a medicinal herbs garden at the side. A cactus garden and a typical Cayman fruit garden demonstrate the historical vegetation during the early settlements.

In the Floral Colour Garden, you will find the typical tropical vegetation, and you can enjoy your walk through the colorful blooming plants.

Another highlight is the orchid boardwalk with its many different orchids. The best time to visit this part of the garden is in early March when the Cayman Islands Orchid Show takes place.

While walking through the garden, you should watch out for the blue iguana that calls this park home. This species is endangered and protected. Please be careful when you leave the parking lot at the park because the iguanas love to hide under your car.

Tropical vegetation in the Botanic Garden

Stingray City

An interesting swimming area is Stingray City, which is a shallow bay protected by a coral reef. Many stingrays swim in the waters and want to play with you. They wait for you to feed them some treats and pet them.

The stingrays are waiting for their visitors at a sandbar. In former times fishermen stopped at the sandbar, cleaned their catch, and fed the fishing leftovers to the stingrays. The stingrays got accustomed to this and stayed near the sandbar. Today these animals are one of the island's tourist attractions.

Here are some interesting details: the female stingrays are bigger than the males, and they only use the stingers on their tails to protect themselves against predators like sharks.

Dolphin Cove/Dolphin Discovery

In the Cayman Islands, there are two dolphin parks: Dolphin Cove and Dolphin Discovery. Both parks offer dolphin encounter packages, and you can swim and play with the gentle mammals.

The difference between these two parks is that one offers a free trip to Stingray City with the purchase of a dolphin swim package. The other park offers a public dolphin show on Sundays.

One of the dolphin parks is on the lagoon side, and the other one is on the Caribbean Sea side of the island next to the Turtle Farm. Make your choice; both are very interesting.

Dolphin with its happy dance

Turtle Farm

Another important animal preserve is the Turtle Farm in West Bay. In this park you will learn a lot about the green sea turtles that call the Cayman Islands home, as well as other marine life like the Kemp's ridley turtle or the saltwater crocodile Smiley.

The fun part of your visit is the enclosed waterpark with its waterslide. There you have the opportunity to snorkel at the predator reef with the brown reef sharks and many other fish.

When you enter the Turtle Farm, you will see the breeding pond where the turtles meet and mate. The female turtle lays down its eggs in the beach area, where the eggs are picked up and put into the hatchery. When the little turtles hatch and grow old enough, they are set free into the wild. You will meet them when you go on a diving and snorkeling trip.

With this breeding process, the Cayman Islands were able to rescue the endangered species. The green sea turtles were nearly extinct because they were one of the export products of Cayman in the past. Today you can only try turtle meat in a few local restaurants, and the hunting of these sea creatures has been banned since 1988.

Green sea turtle

Go to Hell

This is not a curse but refers to a little spot in West Bay. The hell is a quarter-acre area of calcareous rocks. This spot is over one million years old, and the surface of the rocks is blackened by a fungus.

You cannot walk between the rocks, but you can send best wishes by postcard from this place. The post office is right next to the hell.

Wellness and Sport

On the Cayman Islands, wellness and sport are lifestyle elements even in the summertime. When you walk along West Bay Road, you will be bypassed by several runners.

The bigger hotels offer their own spas and wellness locations to their customers and outsiders. Some hotels even have saunas and steam rooms.

If you are interested in exercising during your stay here, you have the choice among several sport activities like yoga, Pilates, or bicycle riding. Another famous sport attraction is salsa lessons or horseback riding.

If you are interested in participating in sportive competitions, you have the following options:

In February there is the Legends Tennis Championship at Camana Bay, and this event attracts impressive competitors to the island.

There are two running competitions: the Cayman Islands Triathlon and the Saint Patrick's Day 5 K Irish Jog. The Saint Patrick's Jog attracts mostly locals that compete, while the triathlon draws both—local and international—participants to Cayman. The triathlon is one of the biggest sport events on the island.

Another important sporting event is the Flowers Sea Swim in June each year at the Seven Miles Beach stretch. In 2014 eight hundred participants were counted in this one-mile swim, and not everyone was an Olympian swimmer. Participation and fun count more than winning the race.

Diving

The Cayman Islands are one of the diving capitals of the world, say the diving enthusiasts. You will certainly agree when you know how much the islands have to offer in this sport.

There are 365 different diving locations around the islands that you can explore. The diving places are sunken wrecks, coral reefs, or caves. Millions of beautifully colored fish and other marine life await you. You can explore this wonderworld on your own or with a professional guide.

Even when you have never dived in your whole life, you can learn it here on the island. The education options start with snorkeling lessons and end with the professional diving certification. The usual open water diving certification takes three to four days and includes diving trips with instructors.

The best-known diving sides are the Kittiwake and the Cali on the west side of the island. At other locations you will find underwater statues like the mermaid *Amphitrite* or the *Guardian of the Reef* or the reef formations with their wonderful coral gardens.

When you do not want to learn diving, you can also explore interesting places by snorkeling with the diving helmet. The driest way to discover the underwater world in the Cayman Islands is to take a submarine ride. The ride can go either a hundred feet into the depth or only five feet under the surface.

Golf

On Cayman golf players will find their playground, too. Even when there are no big international golf tournaments on the island, the National Golf Tournament still attracts many players. This tournament is one of the benefit events for the Nation Trust in Cayman, whose mission is to protect the future of Cayman's heritage.

Golfers have a choice between three golf ground options. Two greens have nine holes and one has eighteen holes. To play a round on these golf greens is expensive for nonclub members, but there are twilight rates offered so that you can for a less expensive charge.

Boating

Like any other island nation, the Cayman Islands welcome boaters. However, based on the geography and size of the island, there are not as many marinas available as you may hope. There are two yacht clubs that offer public boat docks; one is in Seven Miles Beach and the other is in Georgetown.

Private boaters who want to have their boat at their own private dock have to search for a property or a piece of land that offers this possiblity on the lagoon side of the North Sound Bay. You will find more details on this matter in the real estate section of the book.

One of the highlighted events in the Cayman Islands is the Cayman Islands International Fishing Tournament. This event attracts many participants, and you have to register early if you want to participate.

Yacht club

Tours

In case you prefer to lay back and be entertained, here are a few suggestions for organized trips. On these trips you will get a good experience of the natural beauty of the islands and their lifestyle.

Be a Pirate for a Day

The Cayman Islands were always an excellent hiding place for pirates, and the sense of pirate adventure is still very alive here. This sense means fun and having a good time. The best way to enjoy this feeling is to take a pirate tour on a pirate's ship.

The pirate ship in the Cayman is the *Jolly Roger*. This ship is a replica of the *Nina*, one of the ships Christopher Columbus commanded when he was exploring the Caribbean islands.

You can either take a day's pirate journey with a pirate trail and a sword fight or you can choose the sunset tour with cocktails and a dinner while the sun sinks behind the horizon.

With the White Submarine into the Depth

For nondivers there is an excellent option to see the corals and fish without even getting wet: take a submarine tour, and discover the treasures of the underwater world on the open water's shores.

You have the choice between a daytime and a nighttime dive with the submarine or a boat tour in the shallow waters of the coast. Whatever you like best, each trip has its excitement.

At the boat tour, you are only five feet below the surface and see the underwater world at the shallow reefs, while during the submarine dive, the vessel goes more than a hundred feet below the surface. The dive tour moves along the so-called Cayman drop or Cayman wall, where it goes twenty-five thousand feet into the Cayman Trench, the deepest point in the whole Caribbean Sea.

On this dive you get an impression of the changes in the corals' structures and the fish population. In the areas closer to the surface, the corals are more compact and higher in growth while they are wider spread in growth in the depth to catch more sunlight for their survival.

It is a fascinating world, and you should not miss such an experience.

Let's dive down

Feel Your Senses in the Lagoon

This tour is inside the North Sound Lagoon and offers you the experience of different nature areas. You will have your own encounter with nature and marine life.

There are many different tours available, and they are from two hours up to six hours in length. You have to decide how much you would like to see and experience. However, take this advice: whatever adventure tour to take, always have a pair of flip-flops or bathing shoes with you. You never know where you have to leave your boat and how hot the surface is on which you have to walk. You can burn the bottoms of your feet very quickly.

The shorter tours only go to Stingray City to meet the stingrays and to Starfish Point and see the starfish in the shallow sandbar waters. You can take your own pictures with a starfish and play with the gentle stingrays.

During the longer trips, you will see all the interesting spots within the lagoon in one day. The first stop goes to the mangrove woods in the natural preserve, where you learn why the mangroves are so important for all the islands where they grow. Besides the stops at Starfish Point and the sandbar in Stingray City, you will also stop at the nearby reef. This reef protects the lagoon against the rough water of the Caribbean Sea and the bigger predators like sharks. At this reef you usually have time for a snorkeling trip and can enjoy the fish at the reef. If you are lucky, you will see a moray eel. The moray eel is usually very shy and disappears into protective caves or holes as soon as it spots you.

Starfish Point

Caribbean Tasting Tour

There are many restaurants on the island where you will find all kinds of tastes from many countries of the world. If you are interested in trying modern dishes combined with the typical Cayman flavor, you can go on a tasting tour. This tour takes place in Camana Bay, and you only need your feet and an empty belly on this trip.

The culinary journey starts with a glass of sparkling wine in the local wine tasting location. From there it goes from restaurant to restaurant. In one you will get a salad, two others offer main dishes, and at the last stop, you get a delicious dessert, and each location offers a tropical beverage with the meal. The tour finishes at the starting point with a last glass of wine.

This tour is an excellent opportunity to get familiar with the different restaurants and to find out where you want to go for a second time.

Taste the Caribbean

The Grand Cayman Drinks

After you have tried the local food, you should also give the local beverages a try. For this tour you definitely should make arrangements for your way home, because this tasting tour will make you drunk.

You have different tours to choose from, the brewery tour or the distillery tour.

On Cayman they brew their own beer, and the beer brewery tour gives you the chance to taste these special island beers. The brewery produces five different sorts of beer—a premium lager, a premium light beer, a bock beer, a Pilsen lager, and a stout. On the tour you will taste them all.

At the distillery tour, you learn many interesting things about the local manufactured spirits—there are two sorts of rum with more than six different rum tastes and one vodka distilled on the site. After the distillery tour, you have the opportunity to taste the handcrafted spirits of the Cayman Islands yourself and find out which kind of rum you like best.

Try it right from the barrel

Eat, Drink, and Be Happy

Let us come to the most important part of life—food and drinks—and where you find them. The restaurant and bar scene is diverse, and you should make a plan where to go when you only have a few days on Grand Cayman.

Most of the restaurants and bars are on the west side of the islands along West Bay Road and along the waterfront in Georgetown. There are also interesting bars within the hotels in Seven Miles Beach that you should not miss.

Nearly every bar has happy hours where you get discounted cocktails and sometime appetizers, too. Often you can dine in the bar area or find a nice restaurant close by.

Not only do the happy hours lure people into the bars, but the special dishes or speciality events do also. In one bar or restaurant, you will get BBQ with all you can eat or a Caribbean buffet, or you can feast like a pirate. This is only a short list, and there is much more to discover.

All the locations are easy to reach either on foot or with a vehicle—rental car, local bus, or taxi. It is always recommended not to drive after a dinner with alcoholic beverages because the traffic on the left side of the road is an additional challenge in such a situation.

The speciality in the Cayman Islands is all kinds of seafood and fish. You will find an overwhelming number of dishes that include all kinds of fish and lobsters. The lobsters and fish are caught just offshore and are as fresh as they can be, cooked and seasoned with Caribbean or international taste. The best place to enjoy such a delicious meal is in a waterfront restaurant. You first enjoy the sunset with a cocktail in your hand and have your dinner afterward when the sun disappears.

If you do not care for fish or seafood, the restaurants offer a meat alternative. Such an alternative can be chicken or beef, and in some restaurants they also serve pork.

The second favorite dish in the Cayman Islands is chicken—cooked or roasted. Choose how you like it best, and such a dish is always spicy seasoned.

The above dishes you can order in every restaurant, but the most traditional dish—a turtle burger—is only available in some small local restaurants, and you have to search for these places.

The following traditional food items you will not find in restaurants but only in grocery stores and in the farmers' markets.

A special sweet treat in the Cayman Islands are tamarind candies. You can buy these candies as tamarind balls. You should try them. They are very sticky and have a wonderful sweet-sour taste.

Other delicious Cayman products are the jellies and jams that you can buy at the farmers' markets. One favorite and exotic flavor is the pepper jelly. Such a jelly tastes best on a cracker with goat cheese. When you see it, you should try it.

How about diner with a tropical drink?

This finishes the introduction overview about the Cayman Islands, and now we start with the overview of how to buy a real estate property or open a business in this tropical paradise.

Real Estate and Investments in the Cayman Islands

We have now finished the general overview of the Cayman Islands, and you know what to expect when you come here. Maybe you get the impression, that the Cayman Islands are only a tropical vacation spot. However, that is only one side of the coin.

This country has more benefits to offer than sun, water, beaches, and cocktails in the sunset.

The potential of this country is based on its main industry—financial services. Cayman is one of the main world financial centers, and many worldwide active banks and companies operate portions of their businesses from this island.

Let's take a look into today's national and economic details and see how you also can benefit from the potential of the Cayman Islands.

Government Today

The Cayman Islands are an overseas territory of the United Kingdom. That means that the Cayman Islands govern themselves, and they are still a part of the British Commonwealth. The governor is the visual representation of the commonwealth and the queen in the Cayman Islands.

To get a better understanding, let us look into the governmental structure.

According to the latest written and approved constitution in 2009, the Cayman Islands are a parliamentary democracy with legislative, executive, and jurisdictional components.

The legislation and parliament are the assembly with eighteen representatives. The members of the assembly are elected for four years, and they represent the six districts of the islands. Sixteen members of the assembly are elected and two members—the deputy governor and the attorney general— are nominated. The nominated members of the assembly have no voting rights in the governmental proceedings.

The executive is the cabinet. The cabinet has the premier and six additional ministers. The premier is nominated by the majority party of the assembly and then appointed by the governor.

The premier nominates the ministers, and after the consultation with the governor, these ministers are appointed to their positions. The governor allocates in accordance with the premier the responsibility of each minister. That ensures that there are no crossovers with the responsibilities of the governor's duties.

The no-officio members of the cabinet are the deputy governor and the attorney general. The deputy governor is appointed by the governor in accordance with Her Majesty's instruction. The attorney general is appointed by the governor based on the advice of the Judical and Legal Service Commission in Cayman.

The jurisdiction branch in the Cayman Islands is represented by the Judical and Legal Service Commission. The members of this commission are appointed by the governor, and they are selected based on the requirements of the constitution of 2009, when this commission was installed.

The responsibility of this commission is to create a code of conduct and to establish a procedure: how to deal with complaints.

The legal system and the laws are based on the English common law and have local additional statues. With this legal base, the Cayman Islands also adopted the dress code in court with wigs and gowns for the barristers.

This is a short description of the governmental structure of the Cayman Islands. As already described above, there is still a bond between the United Kingdom and the Cayman Islands. This bond is created by the connection to the Foreign and Commonwealth Department of the United Kingdom.

In 1962 when Jamaica became independent, the Cayman Islands decided to stay in the commonwealth as a Crown colony. The term *Crown colony* was later changed to the modern term *overseas territory*. The Cayman Islands are a self-governed country; however, they are also an overseas territory from the United Kingdom.

The visual connection to the United Kingdom is the governor of the island, who has his own flag. The flag is a combination of the United Kingdom's Union Jack and the Cayman coat of arms.

As already mentioned the governor is appointed by the Foreign and Commonwealth Department, and one of his responsibilities as the governor is to preside over cabinet and advisory committee meetings without being a member of either of them. The governor also has special responsibilities for defense and external affairs as well as internal security, police, and civil service.

The governor always has to act in the best interest of the United Kingdom and the Cayman Islands and is closely included into the communication within the Cayman government. The connection and communication between the United Kingdom and the Cayman Islands are always through the governor.

Currency System

With the Currency Law in 1971, the Cayman Islands replaced their old currency—Jamaica dollar—with their new one: the Cayman Island dollar (short CI or KYD). At the beginning there were only CI\$1, CI\$5, CI\$10, and CI\$25 as well as coins with the value of 25ct, 10ct, 5ct, and 1ct. In later years there came two more banknote nominations—CI\$50 and CI\$100.

Over the years the administration of the currency was adapted to international standards, and in 1997 all monetary responsibilities were transferred to the newly established Cayman Islands Monetary Authority.

The function of the Cayman Islands Monetary Authority is to issue and redeem banknotes and coins, regulate the financial services, and advise the government in monetary and regulatory matters. It is also the authority that cooperates with the overseas regulatory entities.

Besides the island currency, you can also pay with US dollars. There is a fixed exchange rate between the US dollar and CI dollar. One US dollar equals 0.80 CI dollars, or one CI dollar equals 1.227 US dollars, and the conversion rate has been fixed since 1974. This exchange rate is the same in all businesses, shops, and banks, so it is not necessary to shop around for a better rate.

If you want to get a mortgage, you should go shopping for the best interest rate. In this case you often also have the option to choose if you want to take your mortgage in US dollars or in CI dollars. The interest rates for the mortgages are based on the US prime rate and have an interest premium.

When you come from a different country with a different currency, you can exchange your home currency directly into Cayman Island dollars, but these exchange rates are floating and change every day.

There is a more stable exchange option available that will give you the benefit of a more favorite exchange rate. We can provide you with that service, and you only have to send an e-mail to the address at the end of the book for more details.

Please keep in mind that you can only pay with CI in Cayman Islands, and a change back from CI into your home country currency may be hard outside the Cayman Islands. Therefore, try to spend your CI dollars within Cayman.

Economy of the Cayman Islands

The economy of the Cayman Islands has been based on two strong pillars for the last forty years—the financial services and the tourism. However, there are aspirations to generate new income sources within the Cayman Islands.

Tourism in Cayman

One of the most flourishing industries is tourism. This industry and its numbers started in the 1970s. At the beginning there were only a few hotels and diving businesses that attracted the visitors.

The visitor number in 1970 was only 403 for the whole year. Today 1.7 million tourists flood the islands, and they are welcome because they spend a lot of money in Cayman and produce a big portion of the income of the islands.

Today the range of vacation entertainment and activities has grown in different directions. When you come here for a vacation, you will be entertained with nature, heritage, shopping, sport, and adventure, whatever you like best. Some of the attractions that wait for you have already been described in earlier chapters.

The huge and growing number of visitors to the Cayman Islands makes it necessary for the government to think about some improvements to the airport and the harbor area. These improvements will increase the income from the vacationers and help with the occupancy of the hotels. However, for these improvements the Cayman Islands are carefully examining the environmental impact and the resulting consequences because the government wants to preserve the tropical flair and the treasures of Cayman, and the waste recycling that will come with these improvements could become a problem.

The Owen Roberts International Airport is already operating above its capacity, and the government is evaluating their options for improvement.

In the harbor there is no berthing facility for the cruise ships, and the passengers have to be disembarked by smaller boats. This process can cause problems when four or five cruise ships anchor in the harbor bay of Georgetown in the same week.

On Seven Miles Beach is a new luxury hotel under construction that will add more rooms to the already existing room capacity. Such additional hotel capacities are necessary because of the expected growth of visitors in the near future.

Cruise ships in Georgetown's harbor

Financial Services in Cayman

The Cayman Islands are the sixth largest financial service center in the world, and the financial services are the second most important industry for the country. The islands have an excellent reputation in the special business sector for offshore transactions because of their political and economic stability. There are no monetary exchange controls, and the earned capital gains are tax-free in the Cayman Islands.

Even when there exist no monetary exchange controls, there are strict regulations in place against financial crime and money laundering. The financial and banking sectors cooperate with other countries in this matter.

The financial service industry has grown over the last four decades, and today many worldwide financial institutions and fund managing companies have branches here in Cayman. These companies generate and manage all kinds of international financial transactions for hedge funds, captive insurance, and trusts. Another service offered is the management of partnerships and incorporations or registrations of vessels and aircrafts.

This is only a short list of the available services, and there are certainly services offered that meet your wants.

New Targeted Growth Industries

Besides the two big industry sectors, the Cayman Islands started to move into professional services, health services, and the film and media sector.

The professional services sector offers all kinds of business services for companies that open a branch office in the Cayman Islands to enhance their global business opportunities. These services give you the benefit of an international office in Cayman without always needing to be there.

These professional service companies help you grow your business worldwide; you only have to choose what kind of services you want. They offer you office space and phone and mail services, and they take care of your annual legal administration tasks while you work on your business transaction and make profits.

The health industry is another growing business in the Cayman Islands. The climatic and relaxing environment can have a positive impact on a person's healing process. Therefore, the government welcomes investors and medical professionals who are interested in such a location for their middle- and high-end patients.

The existing health facilities started their health treatments in cardiac surgery and plan to add treatments for oncology, orthopedics, and pediatrics in the near future.

In 2014 a new health facility—Health City—was completed and has already contributed to economic growth by 3 percent.

The third big sector, which is targeted by the government, is the film and digital media industry. Since 2009 the Cayman Islands have made efforts to attract investments in this business sector and establish the islands as a desirable location for music and film productions.

Already in 1993 the Cayman Islands made their film debut in *The Firm*, and each year in June is the Cayfilm Cayman International Film Festival.

This limited list demonstrates that the Cayman Islands are a great location to go global with your business, and with a business office in Grand Cayman, you are located between the North and South American continents.

The Banking System in the Cayman Islands

The financial and banking services are provided by 210 different banks; however, not every bank offers the same services, and not every customer can use every financial institution for his or her needs. To find the right bank service for your wants, you need to know a few details about the banking system and get prepared for your Cayman Island project.

Forty of the top fifty banks worldwide are licensed in the Cayman Islands, and these licensed banks are allowed to do specific business transactions for their customers.

All licensed banks in the Cayman Islands are split into two categories or classes: A and B. Fourteen of the 210 banks are class A banks, and six of these fourteen are in retail banking within the Cayman Islands and are allowed to work with Cayman residents.

The rest of the 210 licensed banks are class B banks, and their scope of business is restricted to offshore transactions with nonresidents. That means, for you, that even when your home country bank is licensed in the Cayman Islands, you can use their services only for offshore transactions. These banks will not be able to provide you with retail bank services like a checking account to pay for your living expenses. Such a service is not covered with their class B bank license, and you will have to use a different bank for these retail transactions.

The licensed class B banks are often branches or subsidiaries of worldwide active banks from Europe, the United States, the Caribbean, Central America, Asia, Australia, Canada, Mexico, South America, the Middle East, and Africa.

Their business purpose is wealth management, hedge funds, and insurance capital investment management as well as structure financing options. The Cayman Islands are a perfect place for such transactions, because all gains from these transactions are tax-free or, even better, tax-neutral in Cayman.

Checking accounts are only available with class A retail banks in the Cayman Islands, and the monthly account fees are expensive. Often you are required to maintain a certain balance amount. However, the retail banks offer the option to pay your bills electronically. Nearly all companies in the Cayman Islands are using this service, and this option is much cheaper than your own checking account.

The best way to be always liquid in the Cayman Islands is by opening a savings account, and this account is easy to get. The minimum balance for such an account is CI$5,000. However, you need to know that in the Cayman Islands, there is no bank insurance for account losses like your home country may have.

When you open an account, the bank requires several documents that prove your name, your home address, and some other personal information besides the documentation where the deposited money comes from.

This documentation is necessary to prevent money laundering, and banks in your home country will certainly not handle this differently.

The Cayman Islands have adopted these regulations, and since 2009 they have been on the white list of the OECD—Organization of Economic Cooperation and Development—together with countries like the United States, the United Kingdom, Canada, Australia, and many other countries in Europe.

The government of the Cayman Islands has established a control mechanism for the banking system and appointed financial inspectors. These inspectors monitor the financial services and audit all existing license-holding banks as well as new bank license applicants.

With these inspectors and external audits, the government ensures that national and international banking standards are respected and that banking procedures are in compliance with these standards.

No Taxation in Cayman Islands

Yes, you got that right: there is no taxation in the Cayman Islands. For everything you earn on the islands, you do not have to pay taxes. Don't you agree that is very nice?

This tax-free situation is not based on the legend with the ten sailing ships that was mentioned in the beginning of this book. The correct reason for this tax-free status is that in the past the Cayman Islands did not produce many goods that would bring them money. They often traded their products for kerosene or clothes, but they did not make any profits that could be taxed.

In the 1950s and 1960s, this tax situation in the Cayman Islands was discovered by international law and accounting firms, who used this beneficial tax status for their customers. From then on the islands were on their way to becoming a financial banking center with tax benefits.

In former times this situation was called a tax haven; however, the better expression is *tax-neutral.* That means that you do not pay taxes in Cayman, but in your home country, you still have to pay your taxes in accordance with their tax laws.

Here is a little example: You earn $10,000 in interests or gains on an investment in the Cayman Islands. The tax amount in Cayman is zero. But you are a US citizen, and your worldwide income is taxable in the United States, so you have to file a tax report for this income and pay taxes for the mentioned amount in the United States.

Therefore, everybody who makes profits in the Cayman Islands has to check with a tax adviser and confirm what his or her tax obligations are.

Maybe you are thinking, *How will my tax authority find out about my taxable income in the Cayman Islands?*

When your home country has regulations that require foreign accounts to be declared in the tax filings, then they know about your accounts.

If you do not declare your foreign accounts and your home country gets suspicious, it can start an investigation and contact the Cayman Islands Department for International Tax Cooperation for assistance.

In 2009 the Cayman Islands signed an agreement with the OECD (see "The Banking System in the Cayman Islands") and was added to the white list of tax-cooperating countries. Based on this agreement, the Cayman Islands cooperate with the other member countries, but confidential financial information can only be obtained from the above mentioned department and not directly from a financial institution.

Coming back to the tax neutrality, in Cayman all purchases are tax-free, and there is no personal income tax, inheritance tax, capital gains tax, or property tax. There are also no tax withholdings that you may know from your home country.

Please keep in mind, these are the regulations of the Cayman Islands, and your home country may have different rules. Which regulations of your home country apply in your individual situation depends on your residential status and which tax regulations are relevant.

These cross-border tax matters can be very complex, and when you are not an accountant yourself, you should contact an international tax adviser. This adviser will also be the expert on how you should structure your business and how you should take the title for your home in the Cayman Islands.

With the right structure and expert advice, you will certainly minimize or avoid your tax obligations. We are happy to get you in touch with such experts. Simply send an e-mail to the address at the end of this book.

Maybe you ask yourself how the Cayman Islands can survive without taxes. That is easy. When you live in the islands or do business here, you need to file annual reports with the government. These filings are not free, and you have to pay for these filings and reports as well as your business license.

Another example of government income is the import fees and duties. When you live in the Cayman Islands, you have to import many things because the islands are too small to produce everything you may need. For these imported items, you have to pay an import duty.

For a short-term hotel accommodation, there is a hotel charge due. That is the same with your car rentals. When you apply for a license or a work permit, you also have to pay a fee for the application and permit as well as the annual permit renewal.

These fees and charges are the income source for the government and make the country's economy sound and stable.

How to Do Business in the Cayman Islands

The Cayman Islands have many benefits when you want to open up a business and expand globally. The location between North and South America is favorable, and access to the whole world is easy by air and ship.

The Cayman Islands are only a one-hour flight from Miami, and eight international airlines fly several times weekly to Grand Cayman. Most of the international flights come from the United States, Canada, and the United Kingdom.

As already mentioned the islands have a political and economically stable environment for global businesses, and the money transfer is without money exchange controls.

Even during the world recessions, the Cayman Islands did not experience the same problems as the rest of the world. A lack of liquidity was never an issue at that time, even though motivation and business confidence were a problem. That means your money was always safe in Cayman during that time.

The government is responsive and always interested to assist investors and business owners in being successful right from the beginning. Companies offer all kinds of services for your business, even when you are not always local. The technically advanced environment in telecommunications supports your international business transactions, and the banks organize the international money transfers. You will always find the necessary people for your wants.

To take the greatest advantage of this favorable business environment and the tax neutrality of Cayman, you should consult international lawyers and accounting specialists for advice.

The workforce in the Cayman Islands is highly educated. At least 82 percent have a high school degree, and 26 percent have a diploma from a local or an overseas education institution. The business language is English, and that eases the international communication and business transactions.

Establishing a business is easy and quick to do. After the registration is done, your company exists. The information about this company registration is protected by law, and details besides the company's registration date, the type of business, and the address of the registered office, as well as the business status, can only be obtained with an official law enforcement order.

For your business activities, you will need at least one business license, even when your main business purpose is outside of the Cayman Islands. The number of licenses and the license requirements depend on the kind of business you want to establish. This license has to be renewed every year.

There are incentives available for certain investments. Such incentives can be waiving or reducing business license fees, and with a substantial investment in an employment-generating business, you can get permanent residency in the Cayman Islands for twenty-five years. For details on how to move in this direction, you can contact us by e-mail at the address at the end of this book.

When you want to start your company on a small scale with the option to grow, you have the opportunity to use a special business center that offers an excellent platform for your needs. These centers help you with establishing a business, including acquiring the necessary business licensing, business registration, and immigration requirements. All these requirements can be completed in a short period of time when you have the right connections to help you through the process.

We lived on the Cayman Islands and know how to get on the fast track. Let us help you. As a first contact, you can use the e-mail address at the end of the book.

Living and Working in the Cayman Islands

On arrival at the airport, you have to present a valid passport and a paid return ticket to your home country or a different destination outside the Cayman Islands. These documents must be shown to the immigration officer for verification of who you are and where you come from. The immigration officer decides how long you are allowed to stay.

As a visitor you can stay usually for thirty days. This stay can be extended for up to six months when you apply for an extension in person, but the total time cannot exceed 180 days. For each extension you need to pay an application fee and show proof that you have enough funds to support yourself and your dependents.

Residents from many countries can enter the Cayman Islands with their passport and without a visa, but there are several countries where you need a visa. For example, residents from the neighboring island Jamaica need a visa, and when you want to go to the United States from the Cayman Islands, you will also need a visa. The US waiver visa program does not apply in this specific case.

When you come to the Cayman Islands to purchase a home, you can enter the country under the visitor immigration regulations that apply for your home country. There are no restrictions on foreigners for buying a home.

During your visit you are not permitted to work. When you apply for a temporary work permit, the immigration office may accept the application and take it into consideration when you have a detailed justification for your request.

A visa request will be considered when all documents are completed and the mandatory fee is paid, medical information is provided, and the language requirements are met. Such a temporary work permit will be granted for only six months, but only when the urgency and necessity can be proven by the applicant or his or her employer.

If you intend to work on the Cayman Islands, you should not be in Cayman during the application process, especially when you want to get a long-term work permit. The requirements for the long-term work permits for five years are more complex and the costs are higher. Such a long-term permit must be renewed each year.

The existing immigration system is intended to ensure that the Caymanians, their family members, and residents of the Cayman Islands are hired first, before any new person is granted a work permit. The reason for this measure is to limit residential growth on the islands, which has already exploded over the last forty years.

When you start a business on the Cayman Islands, you also have to decide how you would like to staff your company. If you transfer staff from an existing company onto the islands, you have to apply for the appropiate long-term work permissions for your staff members.

Each granted work permission is strictly connected to the requesting employer and the position in the company. That means that the employee can work only for the company that applied for the work permit, and even a job change within the company, like a promotion, needs the approval of the immigration authorities.

Finding a fitting job on the Cayman Islands is not easy, especially when you are looking for a job that is safe, has social working hours, and provides a good income, because you are in direct competition with the Caymanians, and they are in an advantageous position based on the immigration regulations.

The best places to find a job are in the construction, Cayman government, grocery, medical, IT, and teaching fields, and it is always a good idea to get in touch with recruitment companies. The above mentioned job areas are not so attractive for Caymanians because of the low job security and irregular and antisocial hours.

The granted work permit is granted only for the applicant, and he or she can come to the islands. Family members and dependents are not included in this work permit, and they are not allowed to come with the applicant.

When the applicant intends to bring his or her family to the Cayman Islands also, there are additional requirements to fulfill, including specific income requirements his or her job must meet. When the family is granted to live on the Cayman Islands, their visa needs to be extended, like the work permit, each year.

The definition for *family member* is very narrow, and a boyfriend or girlfriend or civil partner does not meet the criteria of a family member. There is also the regulation that in the case of a divorce, the divorced family member has to leave the islands.

Something to note: a child that is born on the Cayman Islands is not a Caymanian. It stays in the nationality of the parents and is subject to immigration regulations.

A long-term stay on the Cayman Islands is limited to a time period of nine years. After these nine years, the person has to leave the Cayman Islands for at least twelve months, unless he or she has applied for permanent residency before the nineth years ends.

The permanent residency is not the same as being a Caymanian. To become a Caymanian, there are special requirements to fulfill by the applicant, and the Cayman Status and Permanent Residency Board may grant this right after the application is evaluated and the applicant meets all requirements.

This quickest way to get a permanent residency in the Cayman Islands is to marry a Caymanian or make a substantial investment in a Cayman Island business. The amount for such an investment starts beyond CI$500,000. For self-employed business people, the income threshold is CI$120,000 and above.

Do not make the mistake of thinking the Cayman Islands are an overseas territory of the United Kingdom and, therefore, the immigration rules of the United Kingdom and European Union apply. That is not the case.

The Cayman Islands are not a part of the United Kingdom, and based on that they are certainly not a part of the European Union, where residents can work in every member country. The violation of the immigration law can result in the arrest and prosecution of everyone who is involved in the case.

If you lose your permanent residency in the Cayman Islands, you have ninety days to leave the islands with your family.

These are the most important requirements that you have to meet, but they are not completely presented here. For a full evaluation of the best option for your individual goal and how to realize this goal quickly and successfully, it is necessary to speak with an immigration specialist.

When you need assistance getting started, we are happy to help. Send an e-mail to the address at the end of this book.

Let us now begin with a few other interesting secrets of the Cayman Islands: the real estate opportunities.

A Home in the Tropical Cayman Islands

The Cayman Islands are a country that consists of three separate islands—Grand Cayman with the capital and the business centers, Little Cayman, and Brac. People who want to stay for a longer period of time and do business come by airplane to Grand Cayman.

The usual flight time from Miami to Grand Cayman is one hour, and from New York it is less than four hours. To London the flight time is about ten hours. That means the connections for worldwide business travelers are easy and quick.

To go to the two other islands—Little Cayman and Brac—which are sixty and ninety miles to the northeast, you have to go either by boat or airplane. These islands are more vacation locations, and they have only local businesses and a small portion of the real estate market. Therefore, this part of the book concentrates on Grand Cayman and its real estate market.

The majority of the population (about fifty-seven thousand) of the island lives in the western half of Grand Cayman, while the more rural areas are in the eastern half. Therefore, the most real estate activities, like buying, selling, and new construction, are also mainly located on the west side of Grand Cayman.

To get a feeling of what to expect from the different areas on Cayman, here are a few details about the areas and the real estate inventory. This is only a short list with the biggest cities to give you an idea of the areas that you have to visit when making your decision about which place fits your wants best.

West Bay

West Bay is the second biggest city on the island with about 11,300 inhabitants. It is at the north end of the western portion of the island.

This area has mostly single-family homes with rural charm. There are also some condo buildings, but they are lower than you may be accustomed to.

The price range of these properties is less than comparable to properties in Seven Miles Beach and Georgetown. When you are looking to rent, you will find some apartments for a long-term lease in that area.

When you decide to live in West Bay, you will need a car for the twenty to thirty minutes' commute to Georgetown.

In West Bay are the tourist attractions like the dolphin parks, the turtle farm, and the car museum, which can bring additional traffic during the weekdays.

Seven Miles Beach

As the name already demonstrates, this area has the most public beaches and is where you find most of the vacation hotels. Many buildings are left and right of West Bay Road, the main road connecting West Bay with Georgetown.

On the beach side, you will find the hotels and condominium complexes. These older condo complexes have mostly fewer than four stories. The newer trend in this construction sector is highrise buildings, so the newly constructed condominium complexes have five stories or more.

On the opposite side of the road, you will find shopping centers and other commercial buildings, and in between you find single-family homes. On the lagoon side, you have mostly single homes, and some of them have a private dock for a private yacht. Another docking facility is the marina of the Cayman Yacht Club.

In the middle of this stretch on the lagoon side, you find Camana Bay, an area that mixes both commercial and residential. In this area's buildings, you find condominiums on the second level and upward while shops and restaurants are on the ground floor.

When you live in the Seven Miles Beach area, you have grocery stores and restaurants in walking distance, and a car is not always necessary. The commute time with a car is ten to fifteen minutes to Georgetown.

In this part of Cayman, you also find many tourist-related businesses, restaurants, and shops as well as some of the best known diving spots, like the Kittiwake wreck.

The property price in this area is on the higher end of the scale and often beyond the million-dollar mark.

Camana Bay

Georgetown

Georgetown is the capital and the business center of the Cayman Islands. It is the biggest town with 27,800 residents. The downtown area is close to the harbor, where cruise ship tourists disembark for their island tour.

The business and commercial buildings are close to the waterfront and are home to many international companies and banks. The tourists have an excellent opportunity to shop duty-free in the shopping malls or to taste the typical Cayman food in the restaurants.

There are also many tourist attractions close to the cruise ship terminals where you can go for a diving trip or for a pirate sailing adventure and much more.

You will find single-family homes in various price ranges in Georgetown as well as condominium complexes with a maximum of four or five stories beyond the downtown district. Many of these homes are also available for rent.

When you want to go around in Georgetown only, you may not need a car. You can either walk or take the local buses. It is also an area for families with children, because many of the schools are located within the city bounderies.

The homes are in the middle price range and are affordable for many buyers.

Bodden Town

This is the first capital of the Cayman Islands, and it has today about 10,500 residents. It is a little quiet Caribbean town where locals and expatriates live side by side.

The beaches in that area are a little bit more original with more waves that bring seagrass to shore.

You will find single-family homes and smaller apartment buildings. The commute to Georgetown is twenty to thirty minutes when you have a car and avoid rush hour.

The prices of the homes are in the middle price range.

Eastern Districts

The eastern portion of the island is called the Eastern Districts, and they consist of Frank Sound, Cottage, North Side, East End, Rum Point, and Cayman Kai.

In this area you will find the original vegetation of the islands with dry woodland and wetlands and smaller villages. The homes are in a rural area with bigger lots. However, when you have to go for a big shopping spree or have some business in Georgetown, you definitely need a car, and the commute time is often more than an hour depending on your starting location and traffic.

The Botanic Garden of the island and natural preserves are also located in this region. You will find single-family homes with moderate price tags as well as high-end homes and condominiums at Rum Point and Cayman Kai.

Real Estate Market Data in Summer 2015

During our stay in Cayman, we experienced that there are many vacant land offerings and new construction going on, and some of the construction projects are nearly finished.

One finished and operating construction project is Health City in Cayman, a medical center located in the southeast area of the island. This medical facility opened its doors in 2014 and has already produced between 2 and 3 percent economic growth since then.

The current business interest of the government is to grow into this medical field and attract more highly skilled medical professionals and patients for their health treatment center.

Details about the medical treatment business and the growth scope are described in the chapter "How to Do Business in the Cayman Islands."

In the residential real estate sector, a condominum complex with sixty units was recently finished in Seven Miles Beach: The Water Colours. The price range of these beachfront condos starts above US$4 million. However, there are other beach condos available below half a million.

A commercial and residential complex is also under construction in Camana Bay, and a new high-end luxury hotel is being built in the northern area of Seven Miles Beach.

Another new residential development is named Ironwood, and a new Arnold Palmer golf resort with an eighteen-hole championship golf course is under construction. This development will include a hotel, shops, and boutiques as well as sport facilities. It is located at the southern shore area of Grand Cayman.

There were several redevelopment projects finished recently, and one of them is the Cayman Islands Yacht Club. This yacht club was completely refurbished and has new dockages and accommodations for 158 boats and ships.

These are a few available options, but the projects and developments are constantly changing, and it is always best to get updated market data when you are in the process of buying.

The research on the real estate database in the Cayman Islands showed in July 2015 the following properties numbers:

Homes	458	US$73,171 to US$35,000,000
Condos	487	US$52,439 to US$11,499,000
Land	571	US$15,244 to US$22,000,000
Commercial	69	US$71,341 to US$10,970,000

As you see there are many land lots on the market, and these pieces of land are all over the island. However, the foot prices vary strongly in the different areas.

For example, a channel lot square-foot price is CI$23.63 (US$28.99), while the usual price for a square foot in a different area is only CI$5.48 (US$6.72). These figures show that you have to look carefully and select your perfect piece of land for your dream home wisely.

You can start building your home on this piece of vacant land whenever you want. You do not have to start your construction project after the closing.

Another option is to purchase a home in a strata community. You buy only the land and select the property model that you want from the developer. They will build it for you, and you only have to select the materials for the house as you want them.

A newly constructed home may be a better option for you because the homes are built based on the actual building code, and they often have energy-efficient features that will save you money in the long run.

Older homes are often not up-to-date and need improvements on the interior as well as in energy-saving measures. The update of energy-savings features is always a good idea, because in the tropical climate, you need to run the A/C every day, the whole year, and that can be a cost factor that you should not underestimate.

When you are looking for office space for your new business, you should know the following information:

There are three categories of office and commercial buildings on the market. Each category has different square-foot rental prices and equipment or fittings.

In the past most of the office space was located in the downtown area of Georgetown. These buildings are older and cheaper to rent, and they are often vacant because of redevelopment intentions in the near future. Such an office space is categorized as class B.

The newer and up-to-date buildings for office space are located in the Camana Bay area and along the Seven Miles Beach stretch. These buildings are class A.

To get a sense of the square-foot prices, please see the following table:

Class A building   US$51.00 sq. /year

Class B building   US$38.00 sq. /year

Class C building   US$16.00 sq. /year

This lease payment does not include building insurance and maintenance of the common areas, landscaping, security, and tenant utilities. These expenses are addional to the monthly rent and sum up easily to US$15.00 monthly.

In today's market such commercial properties offer an annual yield of 8 to 12 percent, and for your purchase decision, a local commercial real estate broker is your best choice.

The market in the Cayman Islands is relatively small, as you can see when you look at the above numbers. The numbers from the MLS are the active listings. The latest closed sales number for 2014 was 1944 transactions with a volume of CI$583,348,225 (data from the land registration authority).

General Information about Real Estate in Cayman

When you are looking to invest in real estate in the Cayman Islands, you are in the right place. A home on these tropical islands has many benefits for you.

You can purchase a home on the islands, even when you are not a Caymanian. There are no restrictions on homeownership. You can do whatever you want with your property. You can use it, sell it, give it away, gift it, inherit it, and donate it without being taxed for it in the Cayman Islands.

There are no annual property taxes, and there is no heritage tax or sales tax during the buying or selling transaction you have to pay.

If you buy a piece of vacant land, you can build a home on it, or you can keep it as it is. There is no requirement that forces you to build on the land. When you plan to build your new home, you have already finished the planning and acquired your building permit, and you still have time for your project. The construction permit is valid for five years before it expires.

Every single piece of property on the Cayman Islands is recorded in the centralized land registry of the country. Each lot has a title description with numbers, and from these numbers you can make a determination where the property is located.

In this land registry, all encumbrances, restrictions, and mortgages are noted based on the strict rules and regulations of the government. This regulation can become complicated, so it is always a good idea to hire an attorney who does the title examination to ensure that you get what you bargained for.

On the Cayman Islands, there are no title insurances that protect against title defects. Therefore, the attorney's fees for this service are a good investment for your safety.

The details for the property purchase procedure are explained in the buying chapter so that you know how the process unfolds and which checkpoints you have to pass before the dream home is yours.

When you buy a piece of land to build your own home, you will certainly get what you dream of. You make your own plans for your home. You decide what kind of material you use. When you make your design and construction plans and calculate the costs for your project, you need to keep in mind that nearly all building materials have to be imported. For this material import, you have to factor in the import duty of 22 percent on the material-inclusive shipping.

Another important point is that, on the Cayman Islands, a purchase contract is already binding and enforceable when you give your promise to the seller to purchase his or her property for a specific price and the seller has accepted this offer. Earnest money is not necessary for a binding contract.

As a down payment for a property purchase, at least 15 percent of the purchase price is appropriate. You should be prepared to show these funds on a bank statement.

For each transfer of real estate properties, you have to pay a stamp duty in the amount of 7.5 percent of the transaction price. Details on this topic are in the "Home Hunt in the Cayman Islands" chapter.

New Condo Complex in Seven Miles Beach

Property Details in the Cayman Islands

In the previous chapter, you got general information about real estate. Let us now take a look into property construction.

The traditional Cayman Islands home in the 1800s had a rectangular shape with a higher pitched roof and often verandas around the house that were covered by the roof. In this way the heat of the day was prevented from getting through the windows into the home. The higher roof also kept the interior of the house cool because the hot air moved to the ceiling.

Some of these construction details you will also find in today's homes. The building materials have changed. In the past the roof was covered with palm leaves and later with wood; nowadays the roof is built with shingles or corrugated zinc metal sheets.

These traditional homes often stand on a lot with big shady trees like sea grape or popnut trees, or fruit trees like bread fruit or tamarind trees. These trees give shade and protect the homes against the sun as they mature.

Traditional home

Because of the tropical climate, there are not too many private gardens with big manicured lawns. The lawn needs to be watered, and water is a precious good on the islands.

Private pools are not standard in private homes in the Cayman Islands because of the high maintenance costs. However, you will find pools in condominium complexes and when you are buying a high-end price property.

Many traditional Cayman single-family homes have only one story or have a second level where the rooms have little mansard windows. This style is changing, and the newly constructed buildings have a contemporary and modern style.

Older condominium complexes are often less than four stories high, whereas you find mostly highrise buildings with the newly constructed properties. Many of these new construction projects are close to the beach, especially in Seven Miles Beach.

The smallest home in the Cayman Islands market has only one bedroom, while the biggest home has nine. The condominium room sizes are between two and six bedrooms.

When you have a boat and would like to dock it, you have two options: at the marina or at your own private dock. There are only a few places on the island where you find homes with the possibility to have a private dock.

New constructed home

All locations that offer the possibility to build a dock are located on the North Sound side of Grand Cayman. The high-end and priciest boating areas are in Seven Miles Beach near the Cayman Islands Yacht Club. In that particular area are still many vacant lots that wait for your dream house.

These waterfront properties are categorized in five different levels. Each level has specific regulations attached, and based on these covenants, the price ranges vary. The waterfront property level one is the most expensive, and level five is the least expensive. To determine which one is the best for your dream home, you have to decide first what kind of boat you have and what you want to pay for your home.

In Georgetown and other areas in the southern part of the North Sound, you will find less expensive homes and vacant lots for your building plans.

When you make your decision to purchase, please keep in mind that not all homes come fully equipped with a kitchen and home appliances or furniture. These appliances and furniture are chattel, and when they come with the purchased home, they should be separately listed with their actual value in the purchase contract. At the closing of the real estate transaction, you have to pay a stamp duty for the real estate property but not for the chattel.

There are differences in this specific matter when you buy a home or a condominium in a strata community, and your agent should explain that to you during your purchase process.

The Cayman Islands do not have natural freshwater wells. The tap water comes from saltwater wells and is treated for human consumption. The water is drinkable and does not smell or taste unpleasant. It is provided by the local water companies.

Many homes on the island are not connected to a sewer system. These homes have a wastewater treatment facility on the property lot. When you buy a property, you have to check what you are buying and how much the costs are for the maintenance of this treatment facility.

With this brief overview, you are ready to make your wish list for your dream home. You will need this list not only for your meeting with the real estate agent but also for your meeting with your mortgage officer at the bank.

Based on this wish list, the mortgage officer can give you an introduction to the mortgage process in Cayman and what kind of documents you must present when you apply for your mortgage. You also get a good faith estimate what kind of costs and expenses to expect at the closing table.

Condo complex

Title Types in the Cayman Islands

When you purchase a property in the Cayman Islands, you need to know a few details about the real estate titles.

Every real estate property has a lot description. This description consists of a numeric code for the block and the parcel, which gives an indication where the lot is located. Each property in the Cayman Islands is registered in a centralized land registry of the government. The government guarantees the title to the new owner with the proper clean documents. In case there are some issues in a real estate transaction with the title, the government will investigate and take the appropriate actions to solve the issue.

The lot is the piece of land on which a home is already built or is vacant land where you can build your own home. There are no restrictions what you can do with your property. You can use it for yourself, or you can lease it to others or give it away; it does not matter. Each of these actions is tax-free, but you have to pay a stamp duty for such a transfer. The only possible stamp duty–free property transfer is between close family members like father to son.

The important point of the transfer is the consideration for the real estate transaction, and the stamp duty is 7.5 percent of the transaction consideration amount.

In the centralized registry, all encumbrances, liens, and restrictions are recorded. Most importantly, it is noted when a purchase contract for a property is pending and that is a good protection for the future property owner.

Commonly a property is titled to a natural person; however, for tax purposes in your home country, or for business purposes, you can also take the title in a corporation's name. In such cases you should definitely seek the advice of an attorney and your accountant to evaluate the best option for you.

The real estate property can be transferred as a freehold or leasehold, and these kinds of titles refer to a single-family home.

When you buy a freehold property, you own the lot, including the building that is located on that piece of land. But when you purchase a leasehold property, you own the house but not the piece of land on which the house is standing. The land belongs to someone else, and when the land lease is up, the building on the lot goes back together with the land to the lease holder. In such a case, it is important to evaluate when the land lease is up.

The freehold properties are usually not located in a strata association community, and they have no monthly maintenance fee.

The leasehold properties usually have a management company that takes care of the general services that are attached to the leasehold status.

The third kind of title is the strata title. This kind of title you find in condominium complexes and in freehold communities where the individual homeowners are also partial owners of the common areas.

The common areas of such a community need to be maintained, and these services are managed by a strata association. The fees for the maintenance and the management of the complex are paid monthly by the members of the homeowner association.

The members of the strata cooperation own the building complex as a whole, and each individual owner gets only a share of the whole development. Each individual condominium unit has a separate record in the registry besides the record for the common areas, and with this separate record for the condominium, the unit can be financed by a bank.

The strata cooperation is governed by an executive committee, which decides in the interest of the cooperation and rules accordingly to the regulations and bylaws. Every individual owner is bound to the decisions of the committee.

One of the decision topics is the maintenance fees and what is included in these fees. Usually the fees include the property insurance, the maintenance expenses, the legal fees to the government, and reserves in case of an emergency.

Getting a Mortgage in the Cayman Islands

You have the dream to purchase a home on a tropical island, but you do not have enough liquidity to pay for this dream home in cash. In this case your only option for success is a mortgage.

Under the above circumstances, it is best to start the mortgage application process before you even start looking for your new home. Such a preapproval process for a mortgage will take about two weeks.

Your real estate professional in the Cayman Islands will also ask you for your mortgage preapproval before he or she works with you.

For your preapproval you will need documentation papers about your immigration status, your profession, and what you earn as well as your overall financial position and your credit history. Your paperwork for the mortgage application can impact the interest rate and the overall loan conditions, so be prepared.

All the requested documents have to be in English, and you should use the approved services companies in the Cayman Islands for the translation of your documents if they are not yet in English. That will accelerate the process of the mortgage approval.

When you start the mortgage approval process, you should shop around at different Cayman banks that operate in the lending business with foreign nationals, because not all banks on the Cayman Islands have a license for this kind of business (see the chapter "The Banking System in the Cayman Islands").

The mortgage interest rates vary in the different banks. The base for the interest rates is the US prime rate, and the mortgage rate is from 1 to 3 percent above this rate. Only interest mortgages or balloon mortgages are not offered in the Cayman Islands.

The usual mortgage term is ten to fifteen years, and during this time you often can repay the mortgage early without any penalty payment. To play it safe, get this detail in writing from your lender.

It is required that you make a down payment in a real estate transaction of at least 5 percent, but as a foreign national, you should be prepared to make a higher down payment, for example 25 to 40 percent.

Many lenders also require life insurance for the term of the mortgage so that in case anything happens to you as the borrower, the mortgage is covered and can be repaid with the proceeds of that life insurance. The bank accepts any life insurance as long as it is assignable to the lender.

When you are looking for such life insurance, you should keep in mind that risk life insurance is less expensive and will offer the mortgage protection that you need. An insurance professional will certainly help you with this matter.

On the mortgage amount, there is a stamp duty due when the money is paid at the transaction closing. The duty amount depends on the mortgage amount. When the mortgage is lower than CI$300,000 the stamp duty is 1 percent; above that amount the stamp duty rises to 1.5 percent of the mortgage amount.

To protect themselves and to protect you, the lender will hire an attorney to do the title examination on your behalf. For this legal service, you will have to pay a fee of up to 1 percent of the purchase price of the property.

For the evaluation of the property value of your home, the lender will order a special report from an approved surveyor. The task of this surveyor is to ensure the fair market value based on the internationally recognized standards of the Royal Institute of Chartered Surveyors—RICS. This report is comparable to an appraisal in the United States. The main focus of this report is the structural condition of the house, the replacement costs, and the actual construction costs based on upgrades and depreciation. Such a report costs about CI$400.00 and is part of the closing costs on the buyer side.

As you already know, the currency in the Cayman Islands is Cayman Island dollars (CI), and as a foreign national, you have the choice between two currencies—USD (United States dollars) and CI—for your account. When you go with USD, everything will be documented in this currency. Otherwise, everything will be in CI.

When you have finished your application process and the lender has preapproved you for a mortgage, you are prepared for your meeting with the real estate professional.

Realtor Association in Cayman Islands

In 1987 the Realtors in the Cayman Islands established their national association. This association is called the Cayman Islands Real Estate Broker Association—or for short, CIREBA.

This association built their processes and procedures on the experience of the Realtor association in the United States and Canada but based them on the legal system of the United Kingdom. This means that there are differences in the real estate transaction that you should know about when buying in the Cayman Islands.

The association updates and adapts its procedures and conduct of business practice constantly. The association has its own code of ethics, and each member is bound to this code and works from that foundation.

Every real estate transaction in the Cayman Islands that is done by a member of the association is reviewed by CIREBA to ensure that all necessary processing and legal steps are taken. This gives you an extra portion of safety in your transaction.

In 2014 the association had 31 real estate company members with 161 agents and brokers. The real estate transfers in 2014 totaled 1,944 according to the official resource of the goverment, and 85 percent of these transactions were completed by a member of CIREBA.

The CIREBA operates a Multiple Listing Service—MLS— where all actual available properties on the islands are listed, and every licensed real estate agent can sell you each of these properties.

In summer 2015 there were 1,585 listings available on the MLS. These listings are serviced by the available real estate professionals. Not included in this number are the properties *For Sale by Owner*.

The CIREBA association has a staggered commission system for their listings. The commission for listings with a sale price below CI$/US$95,000 is 10 percent, and the higher the listed sale price, the lower the commission percentage. The lowest percentage is 4 percent with a listed sale price of CI$/US$9,995,000 and above. The amount is meant as a threshold and the currency has no influence on this threshold. These rates are valid for residential transactions, and for commercial transactions there are different rates.

As already mentioned it is not necessary to visit several agents on the islands, because every agent can show you every listing on the MLS, and you will get the best available property selection possible from each agent.

Every real estate professional has to study for his or her license and takes the license exam. After passing the exam, the agent is entitled to perform real estate services within a real estate company.

Real estate professionals have to renew their licenses every three years and have to attend educational sessions every year to keep up with legal and regulation changes.

On the other hand, you may upset the agents when you practice agent hopping, because the real estate professional community is small. When the agents find out that you are hopping, they may not be willing to work with you.

When you are the buyer in a real estate transaction, you do not have to pay for the real estate services because the seller will pay the commission to the listing office. The listing office splits this commission on a fifty-fifty base with your buyer agent. This commission splitting is regulated by the membership in the CIREBA and is valid for exclusive sale listings on the MLS database.

If you are looking for a rental unit in the Cayman Islands, you need to contact different agents. Rental listings are not exclusively listed with one agent or one office. The landlord often hires several agents for the marketing of his or her rental unit. Even in this case, you as the tenant do not pay for the agent's service; the landlord does.

If your real estate professional in your home country makes the connection to the real estate professional in the Cayman Islands, he or she can earn a referral fee from the accepting agent in Cayman. The referral fee percentage will be negotiated between the real estate professionals.

Home Hunt in the Cayman Islands

Now you know how to get ready for your house hunt in the Cayman Islands, and you have your preapproval letter from your mortgage lender in your pocket. You are ready to go with your real estate agent on the home search and showings.

Based on your wish list, the real estate agent will research the MLS database for the best matching properties on the market. At this moment you will already know if you want to buy an existing home or if you would like to build your own dream home.

The purchase of an existing home is slightly different from the purchase of a piece of land and has a few different steps. These differences when buying a piece of land are explained in the chapter "Building Your Dream Home in the Cayman Islands."

Let's assume you decide to buy an existing property. That can be a house or condominium, and you have to decide if you want to buy a newer construction or an older one.

When you buy a newly constructed home, you often can move in right away without spending too much money for renovation. Everything is new and in good shape and is hopefully energy efficient.

With an older home, you often have some issues to resolve before you move in. You at least have to do some painting. However, often you have more to do than that—maybe updating the kitchen and bathrooms and/or installing new appliances.

On your wish list, you certainly have written what your priorities are and how much your dream home should cost.

Here are some priorities that you should keep in your close focus. You have to tell your real estate agent these details at the beginning of your house hunt:

1. Is the home that you want your primary residence or a vacation home?

2. Do you want to have a house or a condominium/strata unit?

3. How many bed- and bathrooms do you want?

4. Do you want a garage?

5. Do you want a yard?

6. Do you want to have a boat?

7. Do you want to renovate?

8. Do you have children that need to go to school?

9. How much do you want to spend for your new home?

This is a short but important wish list for your home in the Cayman Islands. Now let us see why these questions are relevant.

When the home is your primary residence, then you intend to live in Cayman Islands year-round. In this case you must have the immigration status for a permanent residency on the islands.

If your home is a vacation domicile, your immigration status is not relevant because you can easily come to the island for at least thirty days with the option to extend up to six months. However, there are some exempt countries that may need a visa before you enter the Cayman Islands. If you have any questions on this topic, send us a message at the e-mail address at the end of this book.

When you are living all year in Cayman, a house may be the best option. In a home you can do whatever you want, and you only have to pay for your utilities and homeowner insurance, but you do not have to pay property tax. There is no property tax in Cayman. For the yard maintenance, you can hire a service company, if you do not want to do it yourself.

The maintenance task may tip your want scale more to a condominium/strata home. Such a strata community can consist of homes or condominiums, and the maintenance tasks are often included in the monthly maintenance fees to the strata association so that you do not have to worry about the maintenance.

In a strata community with single houses you have to check, if you own the land on which your home is located or if this land belongs to the strata community. In case the land belongs to the strata, you only get the leasehold for the land. Information on this topic is provided in the strata documents that the seller should provide to you.

In these documents you will also find if the strata community has a homeowner insurance policy and what this insurance may cover. There is a difference in the coverage of the homeowner insurance for a home and a condominium. In a condominium the kitchen appliances belong to the kitchen, and they are covered in the insurance, but in a house this is often not the case.

When you buy a condominium in a strata community, you get a portion of the whole complex. That means the complex and all units belong to all condominium owners. All owners together are responsible for the maintenance of the strata complex. To get this task done, every owner has to pay a monthly maintenance fee that covers the costs for the exterior and interior common areas. Your condominium unit in this strata complex is a portion of the whole, so you are automatically obligated to pay these monthly fees.

The condominium unit that you purchase in one of these strata communities is separately titled, and you can get a mortgage for your purchased unit from a local bank. How much money you are allowed to borrow from a local bank for your condominium purchase is often regulated in the condominium documents.

One question above is the number of bed- and bathrooms. This is certainly easy to answer when you know how many persons are in your family. Each person should have a bedroom and at least one bathroom for two persons.

When you have to decide if you need a garage, please keep in mind that it is very hot in Cayman during the day, and a garage can keep your car cool. A garage is also a good protection for your car in case you only stay part-time in Cayman.

We have already discussed yard maintenance. However, we should come back to this point, because when you are only here for vacation, you will need a service company that will take care of your yard while you are absent, and that will cost money.

The answers to the questions about a boat and school-age children can limit your location options in Cayman. There are only some areas available for the construction of docks, and many of the schools are located in the suburban areas of Georgetown. Especially in the matter of the schools, you have to evaluate the transportation options for your kids. Your agent will certainly help you with these important points.

For the question of how much you want to spend, you should know if you can and if you want to renovate your home. If you are a handyman and you can do some repairs and updates yourself, then you can look for a home that is cheaper because of its exterior and interior conditions.

If you are not that good with your own hands, a perfectly renovated home might be the better choice for you, but this option comes with a higher price tag.

Let us now talk about the price that you can afford, and you can make a quick calculation for yourself.

Let us assume you would like to buy a property for US$400,000 and you intend to put 25 percent down. You have to bring additional money for the expenses for the closing. The transaction costs are usually not included in the financing of a property and must be paid out of pocket.

When you have discussed all the above questions with your real estate professional, he or she will be able to find matching homes in Cayman. When you have found a nice property selection, you will have showings together with your agent of the selected properties.

After you have done some showing, you will certainly find the perfect dream home, and you will make an offer to the seller and his or her agent. The seller will decide if your offer is acceptable and hopefully sign the contract, too. With this signature the contract is binding.

In the Cayman Islands, a real estate contract is binding as soon as both contract parties have agreed to the contract with their signatures. Earnest money is not necessary for the legal force of the contract. The promise from the buyer to buy from the seller for a specific price and the promise from the seller to sell to the buyer for the specific price are enough to make the contract legally enforceable. These promises to each other are called consideration.

With the legally binding contract, you have to start your work toward the closing table. The normal period for such a closing preparation is thirty days.

The signed contract is provided to the bank for the mortgage processing and preparation of the closing documents. The details to this part of the transaction are explained in the chapters "Mortgage Process in the Cayman Islands" and "Purchase Statement for the Transaction."

Home Inspection and Site Survey—
Two Important Tasks

When you have a signed contract, it is time to start your own activities in the transaction, while the lender is working on the legal and mortgage tasks. In this chapter we focus on your tasks that are not in the scope of the lender.

Like in many countries, you should order a professional home inspection and a survey for your future home site. The survey is only necessary when you buy a single-family home to make sure that you know where your property lines are.

When you purchase a condominium, you only acquire a portion within the whole complex. The complex itself was surveyed during the construction process. If you need this document for your own reassurance, you often can get a copy from the strata association or the land registry.

The second task for you is the home inspection, and this task is strongly recommended to make sure you know what condition your new home is in. It is important to know if the house is well maintained and how much renovation or remodeling you have to expect in the near future.

The renovations can easily become expensive because not all building materials are at hand on the islands and must be imported from other countries. For these imports you have to pay shipping fees and import duties when the material arrives at the port.

In case you find damages at the home, you can negotiate with the former owner and make him or her pay for necessary repairs or ask for a price reduction, whatever you like best.

During the home inspection, the inspector examines the home construction as well as the exterior and interior features of the house, including the roof and the foundation.

Based on government regulations, air-conditioning units need to be serviced regularly to avoid issues in the future. The seller has to provide the service reports that state the condition of this appliance.

The tropical climate requires a quarterly pest-control protection spraying for every property, and these services have to be documented, too. Such reports should also be provided from the seller.

When your new home is located in a homeowner community, you should request evidence that the association fees are paid and that there are no open assessments or unpaid charges from the former owner.

Another good idea is to request a copy of the monthly water and electricity bills to find out how much the monthly utility payments may be and to ensure that all utility bills are paid in full until the closing.

For your protection as the buyer of a home, you should pay attention to these tasks and follow up for the results. When the home inspection shows any defects, you have the possibility to negotiate the purchase price or cancel the contract.

For the site survey and the home inspection, you have to pay out of your own pocket. These expenses are not directly connected to the mortgage process and, therefore, are not included in the transaction settlement bill.

Mortgage Process in the Cayman Islands

With the legally binding contract, you have to start your work with the lender to finalize your mortgage process until the closing date. The normal period for such a closing preparation is thirty days.

As soon as the contract is signed, you should provide it to the bank for the mortgage processing. At the beginning of your house hunt, you have accomplished the first step of the process, and the result of this process step is the prequalification for your home mortgage. Now the second step: the lending process and the legal requirements are on your list. These steps are triggered by the lender, but you have to assist with documents and papers.

For the purchase of your new home, you have to pay a governmental stamp duty. This duty is calculated on the purchase price or the market value of the property—whatever is higher—and the percentage is 7.5.

The definition for *market value* in this connection is the price for a property that a motivated seller and a motivated buyer will exchange when they both know all relevant information about the property and neither of them is in a distressed situation.

The purchase price is the price in the signed contract and does not include the chattel like furniture or appliances. To exclude the chattel from the purchase price, every item in the home that is sold by the seller needs to be itemized with a value amount next to the item.

The market value of a property is comparable to a broker price opinion evaluation in the United States, but in the Cayman Islands, this evaluation is carried out by the Land and Survey Department of the Cayman Islands. This evaluation is ordered by the lender as a part of the closing process, and the calculated stamp duty amount based on this evaluation is included in the lender's closing statement. This stamp duty is due within forty-five days of the signing date of the contract and will be paid at the closing of the transaction.

In the Cayman Islands, there are no title companies or title insurance that examines and insures the property title. These tasks are done by lawyers. They examine the title and prepare the legal documents for the transfer of the property. Your lender will engage an attorney for this title work, and the charge for this task is part of the mortgage process fees. This fee is between 0.5 and 1 percent of the loan amount.

For the mortgage that you get from your lender, you have to pay a stamp duty for the registration in the governmental registry. This duty is 1 percent for a mortgage amount of CI$300,000 and below or 1.5 percent for a mortgage that exceeds the mentioned amount. This fee is directly connected to the real estate transaction and is part of the transfer statement at closing.

As a protection for your mortgage, the lender orders a separate market value report. This report is comparable to a property appraisal in the United States. Such a report focuses on the property conditions and takes into consideration the replacement costs and the adjusted building value based on the recent remodeling efforts and the depreciation of the construction components.

This report is done by approved surveyors on the basis of the internationally recognized standards of the Royal Institute of Chartered Surveyors—RICS—and usually costs CI$400.

Besides these fees that are connected to the real estate transactions, there are some smaller-cost items involved, like life insurance assignment or miscellaneous legal expenses, and the lenders usually charge a lending commitment fee.

Purchase Statement for the Transaction

To give you a better idea of how much money you will need in addition to the purchase price, we created the following example closing statement for a mortgage.

In this example we buy a home for CI$400,000 and finance the deal with CI$300,000. The statement shows your buyer numbers on the closing day.

Description	Calculation Base	Amount CI$
Down payment	25% of price	100,000
Mortgage	75% of price	300,000
Stamp duty for transfer/government	7.5% of price or market value	30,000
Stamp duty for mortgage registration/government	1% of loan amount	3,000
Legal preparation/attorney	0.5% of loan amount	1,500
Lender commitment	1% of loan amount	3,000
Lender market value report/appraisal	Fixed fee	400
Miscellaneous legal expenses	Estimate	500
Total		438,400

As you see above, the total amount of the real estate transaction is CI$438,000. From this amount there is only CI$300,000 covered by the loan, the rest—the CI$100,000 down payment and CI$38,400 of additional costs—has to come out of your pocket. These additional costs are around 9.5 or 10 percent of the purchase price.

The total of this transaction is due on the closing date, and the closing date is set as soon as all necessary documents are ready for the signature and the transfer of the money against the keys to the property.

Building Your Dream Home in the Cayman Islands

Maybe you will not find your dream home among the listed homes; maybe the existing homes are too small or too old or not at the right place. Whatever the reason may be, you still have an excellent chance to get what you want: build your own dream home.

When you get ready for your building project, you have to ask yourself the same questions as when you buy a home. Sit down and draw your dream home as an outline. In this outline, you put in your bedrooms, kitchen, bathrooms, living area, and so on. You decide if you want one story or more, a garage, maybe a private dock, your desired location, and most importantly your budget.

In case you want to make your dream house as energy efficient as possible, the insulation of the exterior construction and the location of the windows are very important. You can enhance your energy savings with covered porches and shade trees in the yard. Another option is the use of a sustainable energy source like solar panels and wind generators.

For a later resale of your dream house, a nicely designed kitchen and bathrooms are very valuable, while a pool is not always a good idea. Such a luxurious item costs at least CI$200 monthly for the pool service plus power for the pool heating source. Not every buyer is thrilled to pay such expenses.

When you plan your landscaping, you should prefer native plants and trees, because they need less watering. Fragrant flowers as well as edible gardens or vertical gardens in a condominium are also good ideas.

Your benefit when you build your own dream home is that you will get exactly what you want, and this can be even cheaper than when you purchase a finished home. You also know what kind of material was used during the construction process, and you will have no repairs or maintenance for the first few years.

Now you know how your dream home looks in your mind, and you have to start making it real. To evaluate your preferred location, you should go there and observe it carefully, to ensure everything in the neighborhood makes you happy.

During your observation trips, you can look for a piece of land that you can purchase. This is the time to contact a real estate agent and search for the perfect piece of land to build your dream home. Maybe this piece of land is listed on the MLS.

The agent can also provide you with important land information, like the size and zoning details, so that you can check firsthand if your desired dream home will fit into these governmental guidelines.

In the event that you and your agent find the perfect spot for your new home, you make an offer for the purchase of the land. The process for the transaction is similar to the already explained purchase of an existing house with a few differences.

When you buy a piece of land, you have to pay only the 7.5 percent stamp duty for the land. However, you should pay your stamp duty for the land before you start with your building process. When you finance the land purchase, the steps and expenses are based on the land purchase price and not on your building project. The costs for the home inspection as well as the lender's appraisal do not apply to this transaction, because there is no home to inspect and appraise.

Not all pieces of lands have the necessary underground for all kinds of homes. In the case that your dream home needs specific preparations for the construction, this may raise your building costs. The land survey is especially important for your construction project, because based on your raw outline, drawing the surveyor can determine if your dream home will need piling for the home construction or if you are in a flood area where you have to take extra precaution on the ground level of the home.

An approved surveyor can give you some advice in this matter, and you can decide whether to move to an offer or look for a different piece of land. For this service the surveyors often charge a fixed fee. Such a survey is commonly a requirement when the purchase is financed.

Now you have your piece of land, and the purchase process has taken its first legal steps. While you are waiting for your closing of the land purchase, you can already start your planning for your dream home. However, you are not obligated to build on a vacant lot. You can keep it indefinitely as it is.

With your raw outline, you go to an architect who will assist you with the construction plans. The architect will draw your home as you want it to be. When you want to have an energy efficient home that saves you money over the long run, it is a good idea to put these details like solar panels into your construction plans.

During this planning and drawing phase, your architect will listen to your wishes and match them with the Cayman Islands' building codes and regulations. The architect is also able to advise you if some of your desired features are a good choice or if there are better options. However, during this whole process, you have to keep an eye on the costs and your budget. Besides the material costs and the labor costs, you should not forget expenses for landscaping, window covers, and maybe new furniture. Also, do not forget that nearly every piece of building material must be imported, and they carry import duties of 15 to 22 percent.

As soon as your plans are ready, you can apply for a building permit. The fee for the building permit is calculated on the square footage of your home. When your plans are approved by the building authority, you can move to your next step:

selecting the building contractor who will build your dream home.

It is very important that you check each and every contractor to ensure he is licensed and that he has a liability insurance for at least CI$1 million, so that you can sleep calmer at night and count the days until your building project is finished.

The usual time frame for a custom-built home is slightly more than a year. This time frame includes all steps, from the purchase of the land to the finished home.

In case issues arise during the building phase and there are delays, you do not have to worry because your construction permit is valid for five years from the date it is granted.

In the Cayman Islands, there are no general contractors. Therefore, there are several contractors involved in your building project, and each contractor has to create his own plan for construction, plumbing, mechanical, and electric for his scope of work. Every plan needs approval, and the building department makes on-site inspections during the construction period.

Because every piece of material needs to be imported, you should always request an itemized material list from every contractor on your building project. You should carefully check these lists and ask for advice from a knowledgeable professional so that you never run out of building material or order too much. Such incorrect orders can become costly in conjunction with import charges.

When your building project passes all inspections, you will be able to move into your dream home shortly after a year has passed.

Rent Out Your Property in the Cayman Islands

You now know how to purchase your dream home or build your own in the Cayman Islands, and you are prepared for your successful real estate investment business.

What should you do with your property in the Cayman Islands when you are not in Cayman or when you have more than one property unit?

Those questions are easy to answer. You can rent your unit, which is easy to do. You can give your unit to several agents who can market your unit. Rental listings are not exclusive listings. The agent who brings you the tenant gets the commission for the service. The common payment for a rental service is one month's rent and is paid by the landlord in the event of the signed lease. When there are two agent working—the marketing agent and the tenant agent—the commission is split between them.

When you rent your property or properties in a professional way, you have to apply for business licenses from the government before you start your business. This license needs to be renewed annually, and you have to pay the renewal fee at least twenty-eight days before the expiration date of your existing license.

In case you are intending to go into the rental business, you have to decide what kind of tenants you are looking for. When you want to rent only to tourists and visitors on the islands, you have to add a tourist tax to your rental bill. This tax is to be paid to the government.

This tax is not due when your tenant can prove that he or she is a resident for a specific time and has, for example, a work permit.

Depending on your lease contracts, you have to specify to tenants what kind of costs are included in the rent and what kind of expenses need to be paid.

These expenses are electricity, water, telephone, TV, cable, and maintenance, and they can either be paid by the landlord or the tenant. When the lease period is less than six months, it can be more convenient for the tenant when the landlord pays for these costs and charges a higher monthly rent. For water and power, you can certainly get a separate bill from the utility company so that you can prove to the tenant the usage and let him or her pay for extensive usage.

In case the tenant has to pay these costs, you as the landlord should give the necessary details to your tenants and let them know what starting costs to expect for these expenses.

For example, the starting costs for utilities are deposits for water, electricity, and a telephone line. The usual amount is CI$100 up to CI$200 for each. The average monthly costs for a couple living in an apartment are CI$300 electricity, CI$60 water, and CI$250 Internet/cable/telephone (Summer 2015).

The landlord is responsible for the homeowner insurance that covers the interior of the unit and exterior of the building and the maintenance of the property, like landscaping. However, the tenant has to insure his or her personal belongings inside the rental unit by themselves.

When you rent your unit fully furnished, you should have an inventory list that clearly states what is in the unit so that you have proof in case something is missing after the tenant leaves.

Also, be very clear if you as the landlord accept pets or smokers. When pets are accepted, you often can charge an additional pet fee, especially when the rental unit is located in an apartment complex.

Depending on the location, size, and type of rental property, your rental income can greatly vary. When you have a one-bedroom apartment, for example, in West Bay or Georgetown, your monthly rent is between CI$700 and CI$900. In areas like Seven Miles Beach or Savannah, the monthly rent for such an apartment is between CI$1,000 and CI$1,200.

For a three-bedroom unit, the monthly rent in the same areas are between CI$1,600 and CI$3,400. These rent payments do not include any of the utilities or maintenance fees mentioned above.

With the beginning of the lease period, the landlord is entitled to the first month's rent and a security deposit. Usually the tenant pays in cash, with a credit card, or electronically; check payment, especially with personal checks, is not acceptable. You have to find out which payment method is the best, because the banks often charge differently for financial services.

The income that you earn with rental units in the Cayman Islands is tax free. However, that income may be taxable in your home country when you are a foreign investor. How much tax you may have to pay in your home country depends on that country's tax regulations and what kind of expenses you are allowed to deduct from the income.

For example, in the United States, you can deduct the interest portion of your mortgage payment when you use financing for the purchase of your investment property. This deduction is not allowed in every country, so you have to check with your accountant on this matter.

When you are interested in living permanently in the Cayman Islands and making them your home base, you should consider if the professional rental business can be the way for you to achieve this goal. However, the investment for such a step must be substantial, and the investment must be kept for the whole period of your residency. These investment requirements are checked every year by the government, and if you no longer meet these requirements, you will have to leave the country.

Fulfilling the investment requirements for a permanent residency may require you to purchase several separate rental units or a small rental complex. The rental apartment complexes have fewer units than in the United State. An average-size complex has twenty to forty units, and the occupants are often a mixture of property owners and short- and long-term tentants.

When you prefer to build your own apartment or commercial complex, the government will certainly welcome you to, because this is an industry where the government wants to expand. There is enough construction land available, and the government department for building and planning will assist with your project.

Is this something that interests you? Excellent! We can help you get this process started and make it successful. An e-mail to the address at the end of the book is the best way to get in touch with us.

Your Benefits in the Cayman Islands

We hope that we made you curious about Cayman and that you come to explore these tropical islands yourself. In this book we showed you what to expect and how to enjoy your life here. You now know how to get started and be successful with your business venture.

The Cayman Islands are the most sought destination for offshore business, real estate, and lifestyle, and they will offer you the same perks. With the right counseling partners, your wildest dreams can come true. You only have to decide to start.

And the best of all—the income that you earn in the Cayman Islands is tax-free. There is no double taxation as there is in many other investment-attracting countries.

You do not have to worry about taxes on

- income,

- heritage,

- sale,

- cooperation gain,

- capital gain,

- property, or

- withholdings for your home country.

The information about your business arrangements and your income-related details are protected by the law of the Cayman Islands, and you have to take the appropriate taxation steps on your own in your home country. However, when your home country investigates your financials and makes an official legal request to the Cayman Islands Department of International Tax Cooperation, it will cooperate with such an investigation. This authority is the only authority that will release any of your private information to your home country.

Are you ready to start your adventure in the Cayman Islands?

If the answer is yes, we are happy to assist you! You can reach us at the following websites and e-mail addresses.

• Author website: www.andreahoffdomin.com

• Florida Dream Homes: www.florida-dream-homes.net; e-mail: andrea@florida-informations.com

If the Cayman Islands are not the right country for your business and private adventures, check out our other books about Caribbean topics and regions.

We thank you very much for your interest and your attention in this book. You are always welcome to contact us with questions and notes.

Best wishes from the Caribbean islands and the Sunshine State of Florida!

www.ingramcontent.com/pod-product-compliance
Lightning Source LLC
Chambersburg PA
CBHW050510210326
41521CB00011B/2399

9 780986 252921